Preaching
and Teaching
the Last Things

Also by Walter C. Kaiser Jr.

Mission in the Old Testament: Israel as a Light to the Nations

Preaching and Teaching from the Old Testament: A Guide for the Church

The Majesty of God in the Old Testament: A Guide for Preaching and Teaching

What Does the Lord Require? A Guide for Preaching and Teaching Biblical Ethics

Preaching and Teaching the Last Things

Old Testament Eschatology for the Life of the Church

Walter C. Kaiser Jr.

Baker Academic

a division of Baker Publishing Group
Grand Rapids, Michigan

Published by Baker Academic
a division of Baker Publishing Group
P.O. Box 6287, Grand Rapids, MI 49516-6287
www.bakeracademic.com

Printed in the United States of America

Library of Congress Cataloging-in-Publication Data
Kaiser, Walter C.
     Preaching and teaching the last things : Old Testament eschatology for the life
of the church / Walter C. Kaiser, Jr.
        p.   cm.
     Includes bibliographical references (p.   ) and indexes.
     ISBN 978-0-8010-3927-0 (pbk.)
     1. Eschatology—Biblical teaching—Sermons—Outlines, syllabi, etc. 2. Bible.
O.T.—Sermons—Outlines, syllabi, etc. I. Title.
BS1199.E75K35 2011
236'.9—dc23   2011018115

11 ·12 13 14 15 16 17   7 6 5 4 3 2 1

To Richard A. Armstrong,
who served with distinction
as chair of the Board of Trustees
at Gordon Conwell Theological Seminary (1998–2006),
and his wife Miriam

And to Herbert P. Hess,
who serves with distinction
as treasurer of the Board of Trustees
at Gordon Conwell Theological Seminary (1977–present),
and his wife Betty Jane (B.J.)

With deep appreciation
and thanksgiving to our God
for the joy of working together from 1997–2006

1 Corinthians 2:9

Contents

Preface

Introducing a topic such as *Preaching and Teaching the Last Things* is a dangerous step for anyone who wants to be seen as sane and reasonable. This is especially true in a day and age when more than just a few have taken it upon themselves to offer a specific date for the second coming of our Lord Jesus. Fortunately, however, since those dates have come and gone without the expected appearance of our Lord, those books are now on the sale racks—or subject to even worse fates than that!

But when almost one-half of the teaching of Scripture focuses on disclosures about "last things" and prophecy, to continue to avoid and disparage this area of biblical studies would result in a loss of a good deal of the "whole counsel of God." There is no doubt that such teaching on prophetic themes is susceptible to tons of extraneous ideas, but we would be disobedient to the call of our Lord if we left aside large portions of his Word to us in our thinking and living. I treat more of the contemporary objections to teaching and preaching in this area in my introduction, but for now note that this area of study cannot be left as the exclusive domain of extremists. Therefore, note especially that the uniqueness of the approach I have taken in this book, similar to several that have preceded it, is to do expositions of whole blocks of text, usually a chapter or more. This helps avoid the error of some, which is to make a statement or two and then throw an avalanche of references at the reader, expecting that the contexts of all those citations are well known. So, do enjoy the expositions and see if they are not fairly rendered in our discussions.

As you prepare to begin studying the Scriptures by using this book, I must also conclude these opening remarks with a special note of appreciation Dwight Baker, president of Baker Publishing Group, Bob Hosack, executive editor, and Robert Hand, editor at Baker Academic and Brazos Press. In particular, Robert has been most encouraging and helpful.

Introduction

Old Testament Eschatology

About the Word *Eschatology*

It may come as a surprise for most to learn that the word "eschatology" is a fairly recent term. Similar to some other theological terms, such as "the Trinity," it does not occur as a stated theological word in the text of either the Old or New Testament. Abraham Calovius coined the term in his dogmatic theology titled *Systema locorum theologicorium tomus duodecimus et ultimus eschatologia sacra* (1677).[1] Later George Bush used the term in his book titled *Anastasis* ["Resurrection"] in 1845. In 1909, Shalier Matthews defined "eschatology" in the *Hastings' Dictionary of the Bible* as "that department of theology which is concerned with 'last things,' that is, with the state of the individual after death, and with the course of human history when the present order of things has been brought to a close."[2]

Even so, Van der Ploeg[3] noted that Catholic and Protestant theologians tended to avoid the term eschatology for a long time, until it appeared in some of the documents of the Second Vatican Council (four separate sessions lasting from October 11, 1962, through December 8, 1964). More recently the term *eschatology* has become a popular term used by the media and journalists to mean "the quality of the period of the end," a sense that the Greek word *es-chatos* never had.

Simply stated, eschatology as applied to biblical and Jewish apocalyptic writings refers to the consummation of the cosmos and the present world order as history comes to an end and the eternal era of God's salvation is ushered in. That is approximately how Sigmund Mowinckel defines it as well:

> [Eschatology is] a doctrine or a complex of ideas about "the last things." . . . Every eschatology includes in some form or other a dualistic conception of the course of history, and implies that the present state of things and the present world order will suddenly come to an end and be superseded by another of an essentially different kind.[4]

Some feel this definition does not allow for a great deal of Old Testament eschatology, since God's purpose is also fulfilled within history as much as it is fulfilled outside of history. But that is to forget that the two biblical ages, the "now" and "not yet" (see below for a further description), are just as much a part of an Old as well as a New Testament description of the future and of last things. To be sure, this idea of "two ages" is developed in later apocalyptic writings of the intertestamental period, but the concept is already present in the Old Testament as well, even if the terms "now" and "not yet" are not used in the Old Testament.

About the Growth of Eschatological Hope in the Old Testament

There is no support today for the occasional claim of scholars, such as those made by H. Gressman and H. Gunkel at the beginning of the twentieth century, that Israel's eschatological hope came from foreign ancient Near Eastern sources. As John Bright affirms:

> Israel's eschatological hope cannot itself be explained in terms of borrowing, if only because not one of the ancient paganisms, from which such concepts were supposedly borrowed, ever developed anything that can properly be spoken of as an eschatology. Being polytheisms, keyed to the rhythm of nature, dedicated to serve the well-being of the existing order, without a sense of a divine guidance of history toward a goal . . . they could hardly have done so.[5]

Over against the rigid determinism of paganism from ancient or modern times, the prophets of the Old Testament faced forward in time and anticipated a time beyond the coming divine judgment when God would resume his promises to his people as he ushered in a new age in which justice, righteousness, and peace would characterize his own reign over the whole earth. The roots for such a hope are deeply embedded in the promises of the Abrahamic and the Davidic covenants of old. But they begin to come into clear expression in the prophetic writings from the ninth- and eighth-century prophets onward—the works of Joel, Obadiah, Hosea, Amos, Micah, and Isaiah.

"The Day of the Lord," "In That Day," "The Latter Days"

Where, then, did this hope of a day of the Lord, a future judgment, and a time of deliverance arise? Most will want to locate it first in the eighth-century prophets, usually crediting Amos 5:18 as its earliest appearance:

> Woe to you who long
> for the day of the LORD!
> Why do you long for the day of the LORD?
> That day will be darkness, not light.
> It will be as though a man fled from a lion
> only to meet a bear,
> as though he entered his house
> and rested his hand on the wall
> only to have a snake bite him.

But both Obadiah and Joel, ninth-century prophets, focus on "the day of the Lord." Those prophets who followed them in the eighth through fifth centuries provide an even more complete expansion of the concept. In fact, the Mosaic text of Exodus 32:34 (ca. 1400 BC) may well be the antecedent theology that informed all the ninth-through fifth-century prophets who later developed this concept of a coming day when God would act in judgment and salvation. The Exodus passage speaks of a "day of my visiting," when "my [God's] angel" will act in judgment on the nation's sins. It is not just any time in which this divine visitation might bring national chastisement, but a certain "day" (i.e., a period of time) that will stand out as supreme in comparison with all of the other days in history.[6]

However, if the theory that the books of Joel and Obadiah were written in the ninth century BC is correct, i.e., in the 800s BC, then the earliest occurrences of the term "the day of the Lord" among the writing prophets commences and finds some of its fullest elaborations in these two prophetic books. But since so many commentators have credited this term's early appearance in Amos 5:18, it is even more startling to find that it is introduced in the other prophets as if their audiences were already thoroughly familiar with the terms of "the day of the Lord," "in that day," or "the latter days," usually understanding that their basic reference is to some coming future event or series of events. This is why we would suggest, with Willis J. Beecher, that a most likely source of this hope might be Exodus 32:34, which reads: "Now go, lead the people to the [place] I spoke of to you. Behold my angel will go before you. And *in the day of my visitation*, I will punish their sin upon them" (translation and emphasis mine). Therefore, even before the preexilic prophets of the ninth through the sixth centuries BC, the prophets' audiences had come to expect a "day" or a "time" when God would hold a judgment for all those who had flaunted his person and his law, as well as a time of deliverance for those who were his own.

The expressions "the latter days," "the day of the Lord," "in that day," or just "that day," therefore, came to be connected with that group of events and times associated with Yahweh's coming judgment and deliverance. The New Testament, of course, connects these terms more closely with the messianic kingdom of God, but even in the Old Testament there is a concept of the worldwide sovereignty of God, where he will see that along with fulfilling his promises of deliverance and salvation, his promises of judgment will be accomplished.

While the Old Testament does not indicate whether the term "latter days" [Hebrew *'akharit hayyamim*] means anything more definite than some subsequent or indefinite time in the future, in some of its contexts it is used of a time when there will be a universal reign of God, and his kingdom will be victorious over all (Isa. 2:2–5; Ezek. 38:8, 16; Micah 4:1–4). Accordingly, the phrase came to include a certain but unspecified future time, when there will come from the hand of God both retribution for lack of faith and faithfulness to the word of God as well as times of the fulfillment of the deliverance promises of God. It is in these senses, then, that these terms take on eschatological implications.

The Two Ages: This Age and the Age to Come

The writers of the New Testament use the traditional Jewish concept of the "two ages" some thirty times to depict how the historic present events of "this age" relate to the future "age to come" (e.g., Matt. 12:32; Mark 10:30; Luke 18:30; 1 Cor. 2:6).[7] Since the Old Testament speaks of "the day of the Lord," the New Testament designates the beginning of the eschatological drama that remains in the future as one that belongs to "that day" and "hour" (Mark 13:32). Thus it is not that time and eternity stand opposed to each other so much as it is a contrast of limited time and unlimited or endless time. Just as intertestamental Judaism expressed a divine division in time between "this age" and the "age to come," so the New Testament follows suit and uses the same terms and similar concepts.

"This age" is the *limited time* that lies between the creation and the coming eschatological drama. As such, it is the "present age" or "this age." And what gives "this age" its evil character is not the *quality* of time itself but the *event* that stands at the beginning of this period—the fall of Adam and Eve. Therefore, the distinction that exists between the two ages, present and future, is that the present age is limited in both directions whereas the coming age is limited only on one side (i.e., from its inception point) but has an unlimited openness toward the future. In a number of writings usually labeled apocalypses (such as the books of Daniel, Zechariah, and Revelation), the "coming age" begins with events that may have antecedents or connections with history, but it is eternal on the other end. It accordingly extends well beyond the end of "the present age," even though it might briefly overlap this present age.

In the New Testament, the Greek word for "age" is *aiōn*, which portrays a concept of time that is like an ongoing stream of happenings. It is not circular or repetitive as the Greek philosophers depict time and history. Therefore it is much like the Hebrew word '*olam*, which in late Hebrew means "world," not just "forever" or "eternity." Along this linear extension of time, the New Testament has God-appointed *kairoi*, or "points of time" in the *aiōn*, in which specific events and happenings are located.

The Multiple Perspective: "Now" and "Not Yet"

Closely related to the theme of the two ages is the hermeneutical device later known as "inaugurated eschatology." For example, in the Gospel accounts, the kingdom of our Lord Jesus is set forth as *already* having made its presence known in certain key aspects, yet it is also clear that this kingdom of our Lord has *not yet* been fully realized. How can both aspects be true at one and the same time? Either his kingdom is now present or it is not, some will reason, but it cannot be both present and not yet present without there being a contradiction—or so it would seem on the surface of things. However, Darrell Bock explains that is exactly what happens with regard to our own salvation as well: "[We] are saved/justified [*already*], but [we are] *not yet* saved/glorified." He goes on to summarize:

> But both the "already" and the "not yet" need careful defining, for covenant theologians of the past have tended to *over*emphasize the "already" in their critiques of Dispensationalism, while *under*emphasizing the "not yet." Dispensationalists [on the other hand] have tended to *under*emphasize the "already," minimizing what is presently fulfilled in God's program in an attempt to maintain distinctions [and put their stress on the "not yet"].[8]

One of the best ways to explain the way these two ages work together can be found in 1 John 3:2—"Dear friends, *now* we are children of God, and what we will be has *not yet* been made known" (emphasis mine). In a similar way Jesus defines his work of casting out demons: "But if I drive out demons by the Spirit of God, then the kingdom of God has [already] come upon you" (Matt. 12:28). In other words, it is not necessary to identify the kingdom of God as if it is solely something that belongs to the future, for it has a beginning already in the historic period when Jesus walked the earth, in that he began then to invade the territory of Satan by casting out demons!

The Future and the Past in the Promise of God

As I have argued a number of times in other settings, the Old Testament is a set of books centered around the "promise-plan of God," in which God has set the purpose and the events of history, past and present, for their "appointments with destiny"—including those involving Israel, the nations, individuals, and eternity. And throughout recorded history, men and women have struggled with an intense desire to know their destiny and the future of their respective nations, cultures, and descendants, as well as what eternity itself will look like.

The good news is that there is a wonderful future coming, in which God will bring at least a threefold transformation to this world. He will transform the human person with a new heart and a new spirit (Ezek. 36:25–27); he will transform human society by restoring Israel back to her land once again (Ezek. 36:24–31); and he will transform nature itself by banishing hunger forever and making the produce of the land most abundant (Ezek. 36:30–35).

In addition to the centrality of the second advent of the Lord Jesus to climax the historic process and to introduce the eternal state, the other center of Old Testament eschatology is the prominence and unrivaled hope that centers on Zion, the New Jerusalem, in Old Testament eschatology.

Preaching and Teaching the "Last Things"

It is not uncommon to hear some say that "our church does not believe in the study of prophecy or eschatology, for it only leads to speculation and stirs up a spirit of uncertainty among the people of God." But this claim does not enjoy the support of Scripture.

First of all, why is prophecy and the study of "last things" so often demeaned by some, when our Lord saw fit to include material of this doctrine amounting to almost one half of the Bible? We need the teaching of the whole counsel of God if we are to be fully equipped for every good work (2 Tim. 3:16–17). Moreover, such prophetic teaching, though susceptible to a lot of extraneous ideas, is not the revealed reason why God gave us these disclosures about the future. Our Lord assures us in 2 Peter 1:20–21 that "you must understand that no prophecy of Scripture came about by the prophet's [or the interpreter's or reader's] own interpretation. For prophecy never had its origin in the will of man, but men spoke from God as they were carried along by the Holy Spirit." Therefore, those who gave these teachings to us were speaking not on their own account, but the truth they expressed was solely what God had spoken to them! On this point the apostle Peter also teaches:

> We did not follow cleverly invented stories when we told you about the power and the coming of our Lord Jesus Christ, but we were eyewitnesses of his majesty. . . . We ourselves heard this voice that came from heaven when we were with him on the sacred mountain [of transfiguration]. And we have the word of the prophets made more certain, and you will do well to pay attention to it, as to a light shining in a dark place, until the day dawns and the morning star rises in your hearts. (2 Pet. 1:16, 18–19)

When some Bible teachers and pastors are asked, "Why don't you teach on the biblical doctrine of 'last things'?" they usually respond by saying, "We do not feel competent to teach on those subjects!" But our competency does not come from ourselves, but from the power and the authority of the Word of God, for that is what Paul teaches:

> Not that we are competent in ourselves to claim anything for ourselves, but our competence comes from God. He has made us competent as ministers of a new covenant—not of the letter but of the Spirit; for the letter [not the *graphē*, "writing," but "letterism"] kills, but the Spirit gives life. (2 Cor. 3:5–6)

Thus, if we are to teach and preach the whole counsel of God (Acts 20:27), it should include this large portion of God's Word that reveals what the future holds.

Others might complain that we are not always sure how we should interpret prophetic passages, for we have heard that these types of texts must be spiritualized or allegorized if we wish to hear them correctly. However, it is always best to begin by taking the words of the text in their natural sense unless we see a signal, found in the text itself, that the words are meant in a figurative or typological sense. If one sees the words "as" or "like," then we are assured that a "simile" or a "parable" is being offered, for it wishes to make a *direct comparison* between the subject and the abstract truth it points to. However, if there are no words such as "as" or "like," and yet an animate subject is being put with an inanimate description, then it most likely is an *unexpressed comparison*, called a metaphor, or if made into a larger story or developed more extensively, it is an allegory. Such are some of the rules of figurative language, rules that are not invented as we go, but are clearly part of all writing and speaking, which can be identified, defined, and illustrated in classical and biblical sources.[9]

In addition to these observations, one can always note the way some of those types of prophecies have already been fulfilled if we wish to be assured that the original meaning of the author is to be taken in a straightforward manner, or that what the author has stated came to pass in some other understanding. That history of interpretation boosts our confidence to an even higher level.

For example, take the prophecy about the city of Tyre in Ezekiel 26:1–14. The prophet Ezekiel predicts in 26:3 that "I [God] will bring *many nations* against you [Tyre]" (emphasis mine). And then the prophet goes on to describe how King Nebuchadnezzar, king of Babylon, would "ravage your settlements on the *mainland*" (26:8; emphasis mine). The prophet continues talking about "him," "he," and "his" horses and the like in verses 8–11. Then, suddenly, the prophet shifts from this third masculine singular pronoun with an interruption of pronouns now changed to the third person plural, "they," in verse 12. Why does he confuse things? Didn't Nebuchadnezzar capture the city of Tyre of the Phoenicians?

History supplies the answer. Nebuchadnezzar did attack the city of Tyre on the mainland, and besieged it for what most think was some thirteen years (ca. 587–574 BC), but the people of Tyre escaped from the mainland to an island one-half mile out in the Mediterranean Sea. After that long siege, Nebuchadnezzar did not have the naval power to match them and to finish them off in 574 BC. Only when Alexander the Great came much later in 332 BC was the prophecy fulfilled to the letter of the prediction made by Ezekiel. Ezekiel had predicted,

> *They* will plunder your wealth and [*they will*] loot your merchandise; *they* will break down your walls and [*they will*] demolish your fine houses and [*they will*] throw your stones, timber and rubble *into the sea.* (Ezek. 26:12; emphasis mine)

That is precisely what Alexander the Great did. Frustrated, just as Nebuchadnezzar had been, Alexander scraped the mainland of its remaining stones, timber, and rubble and dumped them into the water to build a one-half–mile causeway into the Mediterranean Sea. He then marched his army out to storm the island, just as Ezekiel had specifically predicted! The text was fulfilled in a most literal and real sense. This should alert us to the fact that this is at least where we ought to begin as we start to interpret prophecy: take the text at first straightforwardly before we seek for alternative, figurative, or typological meanings. However, if there are textual clues that signal the use of figurative language or the like, then those signals must not be disregarded, but used appropriately.

So do enjoy your work in the prophetic material of the Old Testament, and thereby end part of the famine of God's Word (Amos 8:11), for the people of God need to hear the "whole counsel" of God. God bless you each one as you dig into the teaching blocks suggested here as an initial introduction to God's revelation of what is in store for his people.

Part 1

The Individual
and General Eschatology
in the Old Testament

Many assume that the matters of individual life, death, and the resurrection of the body were not on the radar of the Old Testament writings. However, most will be surprised to learn that this impression is incorrect, for ancient people thought much about these matters, as shown by signs of the beliefs of the ancient Egyptians left in the pyramids.

It was probably the removal of Enoch to heaven, the seventh very important person (VIP) from Adam, that started a whole new line of thinking. If Enoch, a mere mortal, could be taken directly into the immortal presence of God (as was Elijah some time later), then the theoretical objections to the resurrectability of the body are moot from the very start. Here was a mortal who did not pass through death, but was taken immediately into the presence of God where he has been ever since. All objections as to whether a mortal can go into the immortal presence of God become immediately passé from the very start.

Both Psalm 49 and Job 19 are two great teaching texts that should give Old Testament readers a jump start as we prepare for these seminal ideas to develop into full doctrines in the New Testament.

1

Life and Death in the Old Testament

Psalm 49:1–20

"But God will redeem my life from the grave."

Psalm 49:15

Death, of course, is the opposite of life; it is the cessation of breathing and the termination of life as we know it here on this earth (Pss. 104:29; 146:4). Life, on the other hand, is a gift from God, who alone controls all of our days (Ps. 103:13–16). The Hebrew root *haya*, "live," occurs about eight hundred times in the Old Testament while the Hebrew root *mut*, "death," appears more than one thousand times.

The people of the Old Testament operated in a culture where pagan mythological ideas taught that the gods controlled what was on earth, in heaven, and in the underworld, the place of the dead. Countering that set of beliefs was the biblical concept where the Lord himself is King over the earth, heaven, and even "in the depths" (Ps. 139:8). Everything is under his control and not in the hands of the mythological gods.

The norm in the Old Testament was for the dead person to be buried in the family grave (Gen. 25:8–10; Josh. 24:30, 32; 2 Sam. 2:32). Those who were landless were buried in graves for the common people (2 Kings 23:6; Jer. 26:23). But the worst of all curses was to be left unburied on the land. In later times, some bodies were burned, as was true in the case of King Saul (1 Sam. 31:12), but that did not appear to be the norm in earlier days except for notorious criminals (Lev. 20:14; Josh. 7:25).

Especially in the Psalms, what is celebrated most is life, a life redeemed from dangers found all around (Ps. 40:2). The hope of an Old Testament person was the anticipation of enjoying God's goodness and presence—even beyond his or her days on this earth (Ps. 56:13). It is Yahweh alone who is the Author of life and the Redeemer. That is why Ethan the Ezrahite prays in Psalm 89:48: "What man can live and not see death, or save himself from the power of the grave? Selah."

But the hope of God's people was in the life he would give them beyond death. Psalm 141:8 reads: "But my eyes are fixed on you, O Sovereign LORD; in you I take refuge—do not give me over to death." For even in death, Yahweh is still there: "Precious in the sight of the LORD is the death of his saints" (Ps. 116:15).

The Lord Jesus himself provides the substance of the hope that not only King David had, but that all who believe the Lord Jesus also have.

> I have set the LORD always before me.
>   Because he is at my right hand,
>   I will not be shaken.
> Therefore my heart is glad and my tongue rejoices;
>   my body will rest secure,
> because you will not abandon me to the grave,
>   nor will you let your Holy One [Hebrew *hasid*] see decay.
> You have made known to me the path of life;
>   you will fill me with joy in your presence,
>   with eternal pleasures at your right hand. (Ps. 16:8–11; cf.
> Acts 2:24–28)

The Old Testament has a fairly large number of Hebrew words with overlapping ideas for the dead. First of all is the term *sheol*, used some sixty-five or sixty-six times. It does not have a cognate in any other Semitic language and is usually translated in the NIV as "grave," but always with a footnote saying "Sheol." The Authorized Version (King James) renders it as "grave" thirty-one times, "hell" thirty times, and "pit" three times. Its etymology is uncertain, but it did appear in the Jewish Elephantine Papyri once as "grave." Both good and bad persons go to Sheol (Jacob in Gen. 37:35, yet Korah and Dathan did as well, Num. 16:30). Therefore, Sheol may have originally just meant the "grave," but then it came to also signify "hell."[1]

Twenty-one times Sheol was located in the depths of the earth where one had to "go down" or "be brought down" to the earth (Gen. 37:35; Num. 16:30, 33; Isa. 14:11, 15). But six times Sheol is also parallel with the "pit" (Job 17:13–14; Ps. 16:10; Prov. 1:12; Isa. 14:15; 38:18; Ezek. 32:18, 21). In nine other cases, Sheol is parallel with death (2 Sam. 22:6; Pss. 18:4–5; 49:14; 89:48; 116:3; Prov. 5:5; etc.). Sheol is certainly not an attractive place in the Old Testament. It is surprising that there is not a more adequate view of death and what happens after death in the Old Testament. But the seminal ideas that are found in the Old Testament do come to full expression in the New Testament. Thus, for the Old Testament saint, Sheol is primarily the tomb, the place where speaking, laughing, and praising God no longer take place as they did in life. It is a place where it is dark, dusty, and filled with bones and where tongues lie silent in the grave.

The Hebrew word *'abaddon* occurs in parallel with Sheol (Prov. 15:11; 27:20) and "grave" (Hebrew *qeber*, Ps. 88:11). It appears, then, that *'abaddon* denotes the place where the physical body dissolves. In the book of Revelation, Abaddon is personified as Satan in his cause for death, destruction, and chaos.

Another word we should consider is *bor*, "pit," which is another synonym for Sheol (Ps. 88:3; Prov. 1:12; Isa. 14:15). Those who end up in the "pit" find themselves in slime and mud (Ps. 40:2) and in a powerless position (88:4). The expression "lowest pit" also occurs (Hebrew *bor takhtiyot*, Ps. 88:6). These "lowest" parts of the earth are pictured as gloomy and cavernous places, an idea that usually finds its home more in pagan associations than in the Old Testament.

The Hebrew word for "death" (*mawet*) is found in other Semitic languages and is the state of being dead or the place of the dead. The Canaanite god Mot, "death," is the god of the underworld. But this too is not a place where the Lord cannot go; he is even here if need be.

As already mentioned, death is the place of "silence" (Hebrew *duma*, Pss. 94:17; 115:17). Another word, "darkness" (Hebrew *makhshak*), is used in parallel with "lowest pit" (Pss. 88:6; 143:3). Finally, the Hebrew word *shahat*, from the root for "to sink down" or "to destroy," completes our survey of the main Old Testament Hebrew terms for death and its accompaniments.

All of this background study brings us to the key teaching passage we have selected for the study of life and death (Ps. 49:1–20).

Delivering Our Lives from the Power of Death and the Grave

Text: Psalm 49:1–20

Title: "Delivering Our Lives from the Power of Death and the Grave"

Focal Point: Verse 15, "But God will redeem my life [*nefesh*, "soul"] from the grave [*sheol*]; he will surely take me to himself. Selah."

Homiletical Keyword: Answers

Interrogative: What? (What are the answers we can give to the dilemma posed by death and the grave in the Old Testament?)

Teaching Aim: To demonstrate that God is sovereign over death and the grave.

Outline

1. We Are Faced at First with a Proverb and a Riddle—49:1–4
2. We Are Presented with the Question of Life and Death—49:5–6
3. We Are Faced with the Certainty of Death—49:7–14
4. We Are Given the Resolution to the Problem of Death and the Grave—49:15–20

Exegetical Study

1. We Are Faced at First with a Proverb and a Riddle—49:1–4

This wisdom psalm is meant as an encouragement for those who are haunted by the power and ubiquity of death and the grave. The language of this introductory set of verses is a call that has gone out to all humanity. This call is not restricted to Israel or Judah, but instead it goes to "all who live in this world" (Hebrew *haled*, "world," is a rare poetic word) (1). Moreover, it includes "both low and high, rich and poor" (2). The words "low" and "high" are dynamic equivalents for the "sons of man" (using the general term for "man," *'adam*) and the more individual name (Hebrew *'ish*), which may signify a person of wealth. Therefore, this psalm is meant to speak to all people, in their common or noble humanity.

In words that are reminiscent of the opening to the book of Proverbs, verse 3 announces that "the sons of Korah [who are said to be the authors of this psalm in the introduction, which probably is as original in the book of Psalms as the body of the text] will speak words of wisdom; the utterance from [their] heart will give understanding."

The contents of Psalm 49 are called a "proverb" (4) in which "instruction" is given in short, pithy, abstract thought. The sons of Korah propose to "expound" (Hebrew *patakh*, "to open") the riddle posed here also by using a harp. This implies that what will be explained will be both a proverb and an enigmatic question.

2. We Are Presented with the Question of Life and Death—49:5–6

The psalmist begins with the kind of question a teacher asks: "Why should I fear when the evil days come?" It is as if he said, "I thought everyone feared old age and the uncertainty of the future and rejection that comes from others in those senior years. What is there available that will cushion a person in old age from fears such as these? Will the heaping up of wealth insulate a person in that situation?" (6).

But even wealth does not seem to provide that sense of security and well-being that is needed in this situation. While on the surface of things this may seem like the "Teacher" (*Qoheleth*) in Ecclesiastes, who often raises questions to get his students involved, the psalmist will in this case provide his own answer right within this psalm. But he wants to make sure that all understand the question and are prepared to hear his answer.

The "wicked deceivers [who] surround [the psalmist]" (5) literally reflects "the guilt of my heels surrounds me." The NIV emends the Masoretic text of the Hebrew, assuming the word "heels" ('*aqebay*, a Hebrew word that reflects the name of "Jacob," *yaqab*) actually means "those who cheat me" (Hebrew '*oqebay*), as one's enemies often do.

3. We Are Faced with the Certainty of Death—49:7–14

Verse 7 begins with the confident answer: "No man can redeem the life of another or give to God a ransom for him." There is just no way money or anything else is going to act as an appropriate "ransom" to redeem anyone from death. People do not live forever, so all must face death at one time or another, no matter how grandiose or poverty-stricken their earthly lives may have been. More often than not, many trust in their wealth, but wealth is especially and notoriously unstable (Prov. 23:5). Hence, we mortals are simply unable to buy our way out of dying!

The wisdom teaching continues, beginning with a "surely" (in Hebrew; NIV, "for"). Everyone, Korah urges, can see that even "wise" persons die along with the "foolish" and the "senseless" (10). But whatever they have hoarded for themselves, they must abandon to others whether they want to leave it or not (10). Even those who have wanted to perpetuate their own memory, even "though they had named lands after themselves" (11), cannot tell what the result will be. Their tombs will have their names engraved on them (11), but that does not guarantee that the memory of their lives will be perpetuated.

So in each case the end result is the same, according to verse 12— "But man, despite his riches, does not endure; he is like the beasts that perish." All too quickly this life is over and the question then is, what will happen to us? At this point, the psalmist is not interested in showing what the difference is between persons and animals. His point simply is that death is a universal experience that overtakes all life, regardless of whether it is animal or human.

So far, the emphasis of this wisdom psalm is on the mortality of all life. Even those "who trust in themselves" (13a), and those who are their "followers" and "who approve their sayings" (13b), face the common lot that comes to all—death.

Mortals are destined for the grave just like a herd of sheep (14). Here death is pictured as a monster that "feed[s] on them" (14b), much as Jeremiah 9:21 pictures death as climbing in one's windows to carry off the living. No longer are they at rest in their "princely mansions" (14e). The problem, of course, is not with wealth per se, but with what sometimes accompanies it: an attitude of arrogance and self-sufficiency. All too often the rich are insensitive, deceptive, and always scheming as if the world belonged to them. Alas, they too must face the question and issue of death one day soon. Money just will not help in this case!

4. We Are Given the Resolution to the Problem of Death and the Grave—49:15–20

In verse 15 we come to the heart of this passage. This verse, like some of the great Pauline passages, begins with the marvelous contrast, "but God." A whole new confidence breaks through as verse 15 affirms our resurrection and future fellowship with God—"But God will redeem my life [Hebrew *nefesh*] from the grave; he will surely take me to himself." The wording is so explicit: my "soul," or better still, my "life," is in the hands of God, if I have trusted in him. My life he will "redeem," for rather than demanding a "ransom" from the dead persons, God himself will pay it for them if they will accept his offer. Here is the theology of atonement in the passage. The grave (Sheol) cannot hold the redeemed hostage, for God himself "will surely take me to himself" (15). This word "to take" is certainly a deliberate allusion to the story of Enoch in Genesis 5:24, where God also "took" that man in all his mortality into the immortal realm of God; thus he was no longer on earth! (Cf. Ps. 73:24 where this same expression recurs.[2]) Thus, the servant is inseparable from his master, whether in life or in death! This is nothing short of a resurrection.

In light of this great affirmation, all else in life and death is illusory. So, to return to the question of verses 5 and 6, the psalmist answers even more pointedly. It is not just a matter of fearing when the evil days come (5), or even a command not to be afraid. Instead, he says, "Do not be overawed when a man grows rich, when the splendor of his house increases" (16). The plain truth is that "he will take nothing with him when he dies, his splendor will not descend with him" (17).

Of course, some rich people count themselves "blessed," while others "praise [them] when [they] prosper" (18), but what kind of assurance will that grant to a man who is on his way to the grave? Death for that one is absolute darkness, for he "will never see the light of life" (19).

Instead, the call for all who trust the Savior is a call to clear thinking and living. The path of wisdom lies in the degree of understanding they have. The Authorized Version and the Revised Version correctly preserve the original Hebrew, which reads, "The person who is in honor, but does not understand, is like the beasts that perish." In between this first refrain in verse 12 ("he is like the beasts that perish) and this identical refrain in verse 20 ("like the beasts that perish") is the marvelous promise of life hereafter with God in verse 15.

So the question of verses 5 and 6 is answered by the psalmist. It is God who will take care of our lives by redeeming us and who will finally take us in a resurrection, much like Enoch's, directly to be with him!

Conclusions

1. Verse 15, which begins with "but God," is certainly one of the great statements of hope in the Old Testament. The future is in the hands of God.
2. Death is no respecter of persons but comes to both the mighty and the lowly. In that respect, man is not much different from the beasts that also perish.
3. God alone is the only One who can redeem life and rescue any of us from the grave.
4. For those who trust him, God will take them to be with him so that there is life beyond the grave.

2

The Resurrection of Mortals in the Old Testament

Job 19:21–27

"If [a person] dies, will he [or she] live again?"

Job 14:14

Almost every person wants to know whether there is life after death. And in almost every culture, people have been burying their dead over the centuries in ways that suggest that they had some hope in an existence after death. In fact, the feeling that this present temporal existence on earth is really inadequate to satisfy the expectations of our deepest desires is generally felt by all mortals, and was so argued by Immanuel Kant.

Although it is generally stated that the Old Testament supplies us with no systematic presentation of life after death such as is found in the New Testament (e.g., 1 Cor. 15), important contributions to this subject can be garnered from various parts of the Old Testament to let us know the teaching on this topic is larger than many at first think. If for no other reason, this point can be argued from the role that such ideas as death and the future life played in the religions of Israel's neighbors in the ancient Near East (e.g., Egyptians, Canaanites, and Babylonians). Even though their ideas were false and unsubstantiated, nevertheless, their expectation of something more than what they had found in this life was almost universally held.

In fact, so prevalent were the false ideas of the neighboring nations that the Israelites were warned not to make inquiry by the means they used to contact the dead, such as necromancy, by which they claimed to raise the dead (Lev. 19:31; 20:6, 27; Deut. 18:10–11; 2 Kings 21:6; 23:24). Death was never treated in the Old Testament as something that was good or even final, for it involved the realm of the unclean (Lev. 11:24; Num. 19:11). Life was the key idea and was to be preferred over death. God had meant for humans to live forever—and then sin entered into the world through the fall!

If life after death was an impossibility for Old Testament mortals, as some want to contend, it would be strange indeed that Israelites were to avoid all dealings with consulting the dead (necromancy) or contacting the world of supernatural spirits in order to inquire and gain information from the dead. The fact that it was possible to contact the dead, even if it was forbidden, was made clear when King Saul went in disguise to the Witch of Endor, with the request that the deceased prophet Samuel be brought back from the dead for a consultation (1 Sam. 28:4–19). Apparently even this witch was not accustomed to having actual success at such séances, for when she saw Samuel come up from the dead, "she [screamed] at the top of her [lungs]" (1 Sam. 28:12). However, what Samuel predicted would happen in battle the next day did in fact take place! Therefore, given the fact that deceased Samuel was still available, it surely points to the conclusion that the dead continue to exist.

Early in the biblical narrative of Genesis, the physical translation of Enoch to heaven (Gen. 5:24), apparently in his mortal body, made a great impact on the views of the rest of the Old Testament. Enoch had lived on earth for 365 years and raised a family, and then God "took him" to be with him. That should be enough to settle the question as to whether a mortal body could go to be with an immortal God and experience immortality.

Moreover, if the Egyptian pyramids were already depicting the expectation of the Pharaoh, and those buried close to his pyramid, to be able to return back to life and indulge in a new life of wine, women, and song, as described in the *Book of the Dead*, in the Pyramid Texts, and depicted in the pictures on the walls of the pyramids, it should not be thought strange that Israel would long for something similar. It is likely that ancient persons thought more about the afterlife and death than most moderns do, for they lived with the sounds and the realities of babies being born and persons dying right in their homes. All this could be heard as one walked down the streets of those ancient towns.

The Old Testament does report three cases of resuscitation after the persons had stopped breathing. The first two cases involve the raising of two of the widows' sons by the prophets Elijah and Elisha, respectively (1 Kings 17:17–24; 2 Kings 4:29–37). The third case is the resuscitation of an unnamed corpse on his way to burial, whose funeral procession is interrupted by unexpected raiders in the land, and who is therefore hastily thrown on top of Elisha's tomb, whereby he is instantly restored to life (2 Kings 13:21). But the point is that all three of these resuscitated persons also appear to die once more, so they cannot qualify as precise cases of the resurrection of the body as promised in Scripture. But in their dying the first time, they did not pass into oblivion or into nonexistence; they could still be brought back to life once again. Thus, when they were "gone," they were not "gone forever"!

In 1966, Father Mitchell Dahood caused quite a stir in scholarly circles when he challenged the view of Sigmund Mowinckel, who claimed that "neither Israel nor early Judaism knew of a faith in any resurrection, nor [was] such represented in the Psalms."[1] To counter Mowinckel's conclusions, Dahood listed at least forty psalms permeated by the concepts of resurrection and immortality, along with others from Proverbs, Ecclesiastes, Isaiah, and Daniel. Accordingly, Dahood translated the Hebrew *khayyim*, "life," as "eternal life" in some eleven places in the Psalms (Pss. 16:11; 21:4; 27:13; 30:5; 36:9; 56:13; 69:28; 116:8, 9; 133:3; 147:6) and the word *'akharit*, "last," as "the future" or "future life" in two other Psalms (Pss. 37:37–38; 109:13).[2] Most scholars decline to follow Dahood's suggestions, but Bruce Vawter defends his views for the most part.[3]

The technical Hebrew word for life after death, or resurrection, in modern or rabbinic Hebrew is *tekhiyat hammetim*; this expression does not occur in biblical Hebrew, while it is attested in the Mishnah and forty-one times in the Talmud. However, Sawyer lists eight biblical Hebrew verbs where the idea of resurrection may be expressed: *khayah*, "to live"; *qum*, "to arise"; *heqits*, "to awake"; *laqakh*, "to take"; *'alah*, "to go up"; *shub*, "to come back"; *'amad*, "to stand"; and *ne'or*, "to arouse."[4] Rather than trying to determine what is the precise date in which the hope of a resurrection first appears in the Old Testament, it is perhaps best to note that there are some twenty passages that should figure in a discussion of the doctrine of the resurrection in the Old Testament (Deut. 32:39; 1 Sam. 2:6; 1 Kings 17:22; Job 14:12, 14; 19:25–27; Pss. 1:6; 16:10; 17:15; 49:15; 71:20; 73:24; 88:10; Isa. 26:14, 19; 53:11; 66:24; Ezek. 37:10; Dan. 12:2; Hosea 6:2).[5] But rather than surveying all of these texts as one would do in a systematic theology, let us focus on a key teaching passage.

Seeing God in One's Own Flesh

Text: Job 19:21–27

Title: "Seeing God in One's Own Flesh"

Focal Point: Verse 26, "And after my skin has been destroyed, yet in my flesh I will see God!"

Homiletical Keyword: Appeals

Interrogative: What? (What appeals does Job make to his being able to experience a resurrection as his life hangs in the balance?)

Teaching Aim: To show that Job expected to stand before God after he had died and then to be rejoined with his body and to personally see God.

Outline

1. Appeal for Pity from One's Friends—19:21–22
2. Appeal for a Permanent Record of One's Words—19:23–24
3. Appeal to Our Kinsman-Redeemer for Our Vindication—19:25–27

Exegetical Study

1. Appeal for Pity from One's Friends—19:21–22

This passage is among those few texts in the Bible that have stirred up a host of opinions with a plethora of conclusions that run the gamut of views. But most would agree that in this text Job seems to be at his lowest point in his pain and suffering, and yet he emerges rather triumphantly. Almost all human help has disappeared. With his body racked with pain, and feeling abandoned by God, he begs the three companions who have come to console him, lend him support, and take pity on him.

Job cries out to these three a double plea: "Have pity on me, . . . have pity" (21). His three companions are called "friends," whether ironically or as Job truly regards them, we cannot say for sure. However, they do not appear in the list Job gave in 19:13–14 of those who forsook him, and these three were called his "friends" in Job 2:11. Job begs them to have mercy on him, "for the hand of God has struck me" (21; cf. 19:6–13). Even the verb "struck" is a harsh one, for it is often used of God when he intervenes in judgment with such severe things as plagues, tornadoes, or the like (Job 1:19; 5:19). But it is also the same verb Satan used when God handed Job over to the evil one (Job 1:11; 2:5); therefore it was God who *permitted* this "strike," but *Satan* who did the striking, and thus was the real source of this "strike."

Job feels he is being persecuted by God, so why don't Job's friends see this fact and offer him help rather than pursuing him "as God does" (22a)? Job had used the verb "pursue" in Job 13:25 of God's pursuit of him, which he compares to the chasing "after dry chaff."

Instead of receiving pity, Job compares his friends to carnivorous beasts who gluttonously chase their prey and devour its flesh ravenously. The expression, "Will you never get enough of my flesh?" conveys this idea, for "to eat the flesh of someone" is used of doing someone all the possible harm one can (Ps. 27:2), or in the Assyrian language, it means "to slander" or "to calumniate" someone. This may be a case where both the literal and the figurative meaning combine to form a single idea. Accordingly, Job wants to know why his friends have not been satisfied with what they had done so far in gnawing on his body and soul with their accusing words.

2. Appeal for a Permanent Record of One's Words—19:23–24

After Job appears to have received no help from the appeal he has made to his friends, he now makes his appeal to posterity. William Henry Green comments:

> In his last and darkest hours he still held fast his unwavering assurance that God was his Redeemer and Friend, and though his body perished and crumbled into dust, he would still with his own eyes see God who would appear on his behalf. . . . These words are certainly worthy of being recorded on the solid rock. No grander monumental

inscription can be found. Job could not have a worthier epitaph upon his rock-hewn tomb.[6]

What Job wants is for the words of his protest to be chiseled into the rock and then apparently filled with lead so that they will not be easily erased. Such a practice has been attested later in the famous Behistun inscriptions of King Darius, where such was done on a trilingual inscription some 500 feet above the plain in the Zagros Mountains of Iran.

3. Appeal to Our Kinsman-Redeemer for Our Vindication—19:25–27

Whereas Job has been speaking hypothetically in the verses that precede these verses, now he speaks most decisively and firmly of what he knows for sure and is willing to proclaim to all. With this word as a heading—"I know that my Redeemer lives!"—Job has now taken an altogether different track for stating his case.

Some want to deny that this "redeemer" refers to God, for they argue, how can God be expected to come to help Job against God? This redeemer, they argue, must be some heavenly witness. But such a view is hard to substantiate when one considers all the facts in this situation, for in Israel's history the Hebrew term go'el has special significance. The word "redeemer" occurs forty-four times in the Old Testament with the meaning "to lay claim to a person or thing to set free or to deliver."

Who is this redeemer? Some believe this is only an allusion to an ancient institution in which a relative provided protection or legal help when a person could not help him- or herself. Accordingly, a redeemer should purchase back property that had passed into another's hand (Lev. 25:23–25; Ruth 4:4–15); avenge a slain relative (Num. 35:19–27; 2 Sam. 14:11; 1 Kings 16:11); marry his brother's childless widow (Ruth 4:10); defend a relative's cause in a lawsuit (Ps. 119:154; Prov. 23:11; Jer. 50:34); and buy a close relation out of debt-slavery (Lev. 25:47–55).

But the parallel statement, that "[Job] will see God" (26), and the fact that Job claims that his "witness" is "in heaven" and his "advocate" is "on high" (16:19), lines up well with the frequency with which the title "Redeemer" is applied to God in other parts of the Old Testament. For example, Jacob speaks of the divine "Angel" that redeemed him from all evil (Gen. 48:16). Moses also sang of the

Redeemer who led the people forth out of Egypt (Exod. 15:13), and likewise David invoked the Lord as his strength and his Redeemer (Ps. 19:14). With the prophet Isaiah, the term "Redeemer" became a favorite name for God (e.g., Isa. 44:6).

There is no evidence of doubt or wavering in Job, for the Hebrew text stresses the word "I": "I, even I, know that my Redeemer lives" (25; my translation). Job's comforters have failed him, but Job like Jacob has an "Angel" who is the "Holy One" (6:10), and an "Umpire" or "Arbiter" (9:33–34), a "Witness" and "Advocate" (16:19), and a "Friend" (16:20) who will both vindicate him and deliver him.

This Redeemer is "alive, living." Surely a living Redeemer is much to be preferred to a dead stone, even one with an engraved message of Job's innocence. This reference to one who is "living" brings to mind the references to the "Living God" throughout the Old Testament (Deut. 5:26; Josh. 3:10; Jer. 10:10; 23:36; etc.). Because God is a living person who is alive and aware of what is going on, Job can confidently rest in his help for resurrection to life once again!

What is more, this Living Redeemer "will stand," "rise up" (Hebrew *qum*), often used as a legal term for a witness in court who stands up for one or the other involved in the case. There could also be a double entendre here, for the same verb is used of God appearing out of a storm. The fact that two verbs, both meaning "to see," occur three times in verses 26–27 may also support this second meaning as well.

But when will this intervention by the divine Redeemer take place? Verse 25 says it will be "in the end" (Hebrew *'akharon*). Usually this term points to the distant future in connection with the events surrounding the second coming of our Lord. But Job may be using it here of the time when he expects to be raised from the grave in a bodily resurrection. After all, he claims it will be "after [his] skin[/flesh] has been destroyed" that he expects to see God "in [his] flesh" (26; literally "from my flesh," which can mean "apart from my flesh" but also "from within my flesh"). We take the latter meaning because Job is so strong in mentioning the use of his physical organs (e.g., his own eyes) that an ethereal or spirit-experience does not seem to match his request in this text.

The distinguished professor of Princeton Seminary William Henry Green, though cautious, affirms the view of a real resurrection:

> The resurrection of the body was probably not present to Job's thoughts, certainly not in the form of a general and simultaneous

rising from the dead. And yet it is so linked, *seminally* at least, with our continued spiritual existence, and it is so natural and even necessary for us to transfer our ideas of being, drawn from the present state, to the great hereafter, that it may perhaps be truly said that the *germs* of the doctrine of the resurrection may likewise be detected here. "Whom I shall see for myself," says Job, "and my eyes shall behold, and not another,"—so natural was it to transfer the thought of these corporeal organs along with this personal identity, upon which he insists, even while speaking of himself as disembodied.[7]

When this passage is considered along with almost two dozen other Old Testament passages on life after death, it is no stretch of one's exegesis to see that Job firmly believes that he will rise again to face his Lord and hear his words of vindication and deliverance. He looks forward to a bodily resurrection!

Conclusions

1. A real and personal afterlife was assumed by the Israelites as a naturally and necessary conclusion to this present life, similar to what is evidenced throughout the ancient Near Eastern cultures in their burial practices and writings.
2. Believers have a right to expect that their "Living Redeemer" will "in the end" raise them back to physical life again.
3. Job's references to "skin," "flesh," and "eyes" make it clear that the Old Testament believers were not expecting a resurrection of a disembodied state, or a ghostly appearance, but one with a bodily identity.

Part 2

The Nation Israel in Old Testament Eschatology

O ne of the most hotly debated topics in the Old Testament doctrine of "last things" is whether the promise of the land originally given to Israel is still valid, or whether Israel forfeited that gift when she failed to keep her end of the covenant. If the promise of God in the covenant was a bilateral and conditional promise, depending on Israel's obedience, then she clearly failed the terms of the covenant and the gift of the land can be spiritualized and made over to the church in what is known as "supersessionism" or "replacement theology."

However, if the covenant God made with Abraham, Isaac, Jacob, and David was not a bilateral or conditional covenant, but a unilateral and unconditional covenant offered in the grace of God totally based on God's faithfulness, then the three texts that follow magnify that claim: Jeremiah 32, Ezekiel 37, and Zechariah 10.

After you have worked through these chapters and their parallel teachings, answer the following question: what is your judgment on this huge question of God's promise of the land in the covenant? This question goes to the heart of what the church's relationship is to the ancient promise-plan of God and what way the people of Israel are related, or not related, to the church.

3

The Everlasting Promises Made to Israel

Jeremiah 32:27–44

> "I [God] will surely gather them [Israel] from all the lands."
>
> Jeremiah 32:37

One of the most graphic prophecies of the regathering of Israel back into the land previously occupied by the Canaanites is the word God gave Jeremiah in chapter 32 of his book. He was instructed by God to purchase a field owned by his own family in Anathoth (though they were not as cordial to Jeremiah as one would have expected; Jer. 11:21–27), a priestly town just two miles or so north of Jerusalem. Apparently the family had gotten into financial trouble and were now depending on Jeremiah to redeem the land so it could stay in the family. This type of legal transaction, called the right of redemption, with its policy of redeeming family property by a family member, had been prescribed by Moses in Leviticus 25:25.

The prophet was told that his cousin Hanamel, son of his Uncle Shallum, would come and ask him to purchase the field at Anathoth (32:7). As God had forewarned, Hanamel came; therefore, Jeremiah was assured this request was from the Lord.

True, this was an excellent time to purchase real estate, for prices were depressed, seeing that Nebuchadnezzar of Babylon was currently besieging the city of Jerusalem (32:2); but it was simultaneously a poor time to buy land, since it all was going to be in the hands of the Babylonians shortly! But God wanted Jeremiah, and all who would subsequently read about this, to know that the Babylonian takeover of Judah was not the way the story would end; for Israel would one day return to that same land. Therefore, Jeremiah was to buy his priestly ancestral home in Anathoth against that future day of return.

Jeremiah was thoroughly human, as can be seen in his questioning such a purchase under such bizarre circumstances indicated in his actions and prayer in verses 16–25. But that prayer and those complaints came after he had obeyed and purchased the field.

The Babylonian siege, which had begun in the ninth year of King Zedekiah, was briefly lifted in the Judean king's tenth year (588 BC), as Babylon heard rumors of the approach of the Egyptian army to relieve the Judeans. But when the Egyptians decided against engaging in such a battle, the Babylonian siege was reimposed on Jerusalem.

During that break in the siege, Jeremiah decided to go to Anathoth to inspect what he had just purchased; but Jeremiah was jailed on a trumped-up charge that he was instead using this as a front to defect to the enemy. The prophet was beaten, taunted, and jailed by a now nervous Judean government (37:11–16).

This prophecy belongs to the great section of Jeremiah's prophecy that features hope and consolation—Jeremiah 30–34. We are astounded by the obedience of Jeremiah. He first proclaims the divine word of hope in 32:15 before he indicates any personal doubts or misgivings he might have. Thus he intones, "For this is what the LORD Almighty, the God of Israel, says: Houses, fields and vineyards will again be bought in this land."

That was the divine explanation for the strange purchase of real estate made under such extraordinary circumstances. Only then did Jeremiah voice his consternation at such a strange divine request in his long prayer in verses 17–25. But here is the heart of Jeremiah's theology: his faith takes precedence over his questions. Thus, Jeremiah begins with a sigh, "Ah Sovereign LORD," but he backs it up with "Nothing is too hard[/miraculous/difficult/wonderful] for you" (17). Therefore, while faith does at times involve raising questions, faith also involves simultaneous risk-taking, and venturing out on the surety of the word of God, despite our puzzlement at times.

The Promise of the Return of Israel to Her Land

Text: Jeremiah 32:27–44

Title: "The Promise of the Return of Israel to Her Land"

Focal Point: Verse 37, "I [God] will surely gather them [Israel] from all the lands where I banish them in my furious anger and great wrath; I will bring them back to this place [where Jeremiah lived] and let them live in safety."

Homiletical Keyword: Promises

Interrogative: What? (What are the promises God has made to Israel about her reinhabiting her land?)

Teaching Aim: To demonstrate God's commitment to his promises.

Outline

1. God Will Deal with Israel's Unconfessed Sin—32:27–36
2. God Will Return the Captives to Their Land—32:37a
3. God Will Allow Israel to Live in Safety—32:37b
4. God Will Reiterate Two Items from His Covenant with Israel—32:38
5. God Will Give Israel Singleness of Heart and Action—32:39
6. God Will Make an Eternal Covenant with Israel—32:40
7. God Will Rejoice in Doing Good to Israel—32:41a
8. God Will Plant Israel in the Land—32:41b–44

Exegetical Study

1. God Will Deal with Israel's Unconfessed Sin—32:27–36

God announces himself as the great "I am," who is not only the "LORD" but "the God of all mankind" (27a). As such, he repeats Jeremiah's affirmation (17) by saying: "Is anything too hard[/miraculous/difficult/wonderful] for me?" (27b). The God of all humanity has a center to his plan, which is the promise of a Seed, a land, and the gospel (Gen. 12:2–4), so that all the earth might be blessed—not just Israel!

When God asks if anything is "too hard" or "too difficult" for him, he reminds Jeremiah and Israel that this is one of his names: "Wonderful" (Hebrew *pele'*, Isa. 9:6—"Wonderful Counselor").

This name declares that our God is the One who does wonderful or difficult acts on behalf of his people. This title appears some thirteen times in the Old Testament, as, for example, when the Lord speaks to Sarah in Genesis 18:13–14 and tells her she is to have a child at the age of ninety; or when he speaks to Samson's parents in Judges 13:18; or in Psalm 136:4 ("To him who alone does great wonders, / His love endures forever"); or when he promises Israel's restoration to her land in Zechariah 8:6. Our Lord can do the unexpected and simply astonish us by his marvelous intervention in our often helpless state.

But in verses 28–36, God must just as wondrously deal with unconfessed and cherished sin. God's people had long provoked him to anger and wrath by their "burning incense on the roofs [of their houses] to Baal and by pouring out drink offerings to other gods" (29). In fact, ever since Israel and Judah's youth, they had "done nothing but evil in [God's] sight" (30a). Moreover, they, both northern and southern tribes, had "done nothing but provoked [God] with what their hands had made" (30c). The Israelites had "turned their backs to [the LORD] and not their faces; though [God had] taught them again and again, they would not listen or respond to discipline" (33). Instead, Israel "set up their abominable idols in the house that bears my Name and defiled it" (34). Worse still is the fact that "they built high places for Baal in the Valley of Ben Hinnom to sacrifice their sons and daughters to Molech, though [God] never commanded [it], nor did it enter [his] mind, that they should do such a detestable thing and so make Judah sin" (35). Molech is probably a deformation of the Hebrew word *melek*, for "king," including the vowels from the Hebrew word *boshet*, "shame." In this way utter contempt is expressed for this god of the ancient Near East. During the days of King Ahaz in Judah (and following), Israelites caused their sons to roll down the arms of this deity and into his open mouth only to be greeted by a fire raging in the pot belly of this image! Parallel expressions appear in Jeremiah 7:31 and 19:5. It was the epitome of savage idolatry and a turning away from God.

Some are disappointed that God would show such anger and wrath toward Israel. Should he not, as a God of love, let bygones be bygones if he truly loves people and forgives sin? But this is to misunderstand the nature of real anger: it is not an emotion offered in an attempt to "get even." Rather, it is an emotion of the soul stirred by its desire to see good, justice, and righteousness triumph. It is a sign that something is malfunctioning in us when we can be in the presence of evil and not be adversely affected by it, or not feel a strong desire for what is true, just, right, and good to replace that wrong.

A God who is not excited by the presence of sin cannot be counted on to see that justice is done. In that case, wrong forever might just as easily be dominant and on the throne of the universe. But thanks be to God, he will not be passive to any form of evil, much less to such blatant, in-your-face substitutions for the Living God as Baal and Molech!

2. God Will Return the Captives to Their Land—32:37a

A divine demonstration of God's wonderfulness can be seen in the seven promises that follow immediately in this chapter. Given the fact that our Lord was so distressed with the persistence of Israel's sin, one might think that he would announce he was through with this people and was thereby terminating his covenant with them. However, this never was a bilateral covenant, in which if Israel defaulted on her side of the covenant, then God would be freed of his obligation to continue with what he had promised. The covenant God made with Adam and Eve, Shem, Abraham, and David was a unilateral covenant, one in which he was the only one obligated to maintain it (e.g., Gen. 15:1–6).

What would move God to keep his promise to Israel about the "land" except his own character and word? Surely the people had done just about everything in the book to make themselves as unattractive and undesirable as possible. Moreover, it is in the very same context that God acknowledges the depth of Israel's sin that he also repeats his promise to return Israel back to the land.

The return will not come solely from Babylon, but from "all the lands where [God will] banish them in [his] furious anger and great wrath" (37). These words of promise, then, could not have been intended to mean Judah's return from the Babylonian captivity, for that return was not from "all the lands." This would be a return from a worldwide dispersion.

3. God Will Allow Israel to Live in Safety—32:37b

This future return would not be like anything that Israel had known in the past, for when the people returned from their previous two returns, they had no peace or rest. But in this return, "Israel will live in safety alone," a promise made in the Mosaic covenant (Deut. 33:28), later reiterated in the prophets when Jeremiah predicts this would be effective "in [Messiah's] days" (Jer. 23:6).

The promise of living in safety has a number of dimensions to it. In Leviticus 25:18–19, it involves security from famine, as the field yields its increases for those who are obedient to the Lord. In Leviticus 26:4–8 it includes security from attacks from wild animals and neighboring enemies. But this promise is also enlarged to a promise of *shalom* in Leviticus 26:6, a case for the totality of one's well-being. In addition to these ideas for "safety" or "security" (5; Hebrew *betakh*), there is the promise of the administration of justice for the poor (Isa. 14:30) and a "confidence" in a covenant of peace (Ezek. 34:25–29).

4. God Will Reiterate Two Items from His Covenant with Israel—32:38

Two items are rehearsed once again from the tripartite formula of the promise-plan of God: "They will be my people, and I will be their God" (38). The only part of the tripartite covenant formula missing here is "I will dwell among them."

The stress once again is on the divine initiative that is present from the very beginning of this covenant. This three-part formula of the covenant recurs throughout both testaments almost fifty times. Amazingly, despite the snubbing that the people of Israel gave God, God here once again adopts Israel as his own people and declares that he, not Baal or Molech, will be their God. This is astounding when judged by any normal criteria. It surely highlights the grace of God.

5. God Will Give Israel Singleness of Heart and Action—32:39

The gift of "one heart and one way" (39; my translation), means that no longer will there be vacillations between competing loyalties, for all Israel will be transformed. Instead of having a divided heart, the people will have a deep respect for the Lord and for his name (Ps. 86:11).

For those who evidence such singleness of heart, you can be sure their hearts have been circumcised (Deut. 10:16; 30:6). This is what the prophet Ezekiel means when he too speaks of God's new provision of an undivided heart and a new spirit as the old heart of stone is removed and a heart of flesh is supplied instead (Ezek. 11:19–20;

36:26–27). This is why it is now possible for God to write his law on their hearts (Jer. 31:33). Israel has to be given a heart to know the Lord (Jer. 24:7). In this way, God will intervene so that his people will be inwardly transformed, so they will be unequivocally committed to the Lord. While this singleness of heart can only be partially accomplished on earth, it will be the goal God's people must constantly strive for (John 17:21–23).

6. God Will Make an Eternal Covenant with Israel—32:40

The "new covenant" of Jeremiah 31:31–34 is here labeled an "everlasting covenant" (40a). The term "everlasting covenant" is found eighteen times in the Old Testament (e.g., Isa. 55:3; 61:8; Jer. 32:40; 50:5; Ezek. 16:60; 37:26). Of course, all covenants were meant to be perpetually binding, but Israel and Judah had so violently violated the Mosaic covenant that they had also fallen under the curse of the covenant. Therefore, when the Lord once again restores his people to their land, he emphasizes the fact that the covenant is still in operation by calling it an everlasting covenant. Therefore, he stresses that he will "never stop (Hebrew *shub*, "to turn away [from]") doing good to them," for he will "inspire [Hebrew *natan*, "give, set"] them to fear [him], so that they will never turn away [Hebrew *sur*, "to change course, direction"] from [the LORD]" (Jer. 32:40b–d). God pledges his constancy and watch-care over Israel.

7. God Will Rejoice in Doing Good to Israel—32:41a

Not only will Israel derive enormous benefits from God's faithfulness to his covenant, but God will also look over his newly created people and pronounce it all "very good" (41a; my translation), as he once did when he created the world. This language of goodness does indeed hearken back to Genesis 1:31. The Lord not only enjoys pronouncing good on Israel, but he also rejoices over them, or on account of them.

All of this signals a whole new day for the Lord himself as well as for Israel. What had begun as a strong statement of God's anger, wrath, and indignation now ends in him also finding satisfaction in ending his anger and wrath as the people are given a new heart so that they will never turn away from their Lord anymore!

The "good" that God promises here will not only let them live in "safety" (37; also 23:6; 33:16), but will be a "good" for them that extends through all their generations (39). No longer, then, will God need to draw back from doing good to Israel.

8. God Will Plant Israel in the Land—32:41b–44

Because God will be faithful to his ancient promise, he will "plant them in this land" (41b) that he had sworn to their ancestors (Jer. 3:18; 7:7; 11:3–5; 30:3). While none of God's previous promises had ever been halfhearted, neither is this one. But to add even more emphasis to what he says he will do in this regard, God adds that he will plant them in their land "with all [his] heart and soul" (41c). This is the only time this expression is used of God in the Bible, whereas it normally denotes the response required by God of his people (e.g., Deut. 6:5). God's asseveration here is similar to a human saying at a lower level: "cross my heart and hope to die" if I do not do what I said I would!

In the final verses of this chapter (42–44), the Lord reminds Israel that just as certainly as he threatened and brought judgment, so will he fulfill his promise. Therefore, as God had brought "calamity[/evil/ disaster]" (Hebrew ra'ah), so will he bring all the "prosperity[/good]" he has promised them (42).

To round out the chapter, Jeremiah returns to the matter he began with: the matter of buying and selling the land (43). God had permitted the land to be handed over to the Babylonians, but in spite of that, God reiterates his promise that the once abandoned countryside would be reinhabited as Babylon finishes her divinely assigned job of punishing the people of Israel in a foreign land of captivity. No time interval is given, but surely punishment came before the return to the land of Israel.

In a list that begins with the tribal area of Benjamin (probably because the issue began with Jeremiah's purchasing of Anathoth, Benjamin), along with the villages around Jerusalem, the towns of Judah, the towns of the hill country, the western foothills, and the Negev in the south, it is promised that fields will once again be bought and deeds signed and witnessed. Similar lists occur in Jeremiah 17:26 and 33:13. So Jeremiah's purchase in Anathoth is a sure sign that land in Israel will once more be bought and sold sometime after it is vacated because of the Babylonian exile. God "will restore [Israel's] fortunes" (44). A final "declares the LORD" grounds the promise of God in his ancient promise that can be absolutely counted on in the future.

Conclusions

1. Nothing, not even the restoration of Israel back to her land, is impossible for God. God can do anything except deny himself or fail to do what he has promised.
2. The worldwide dispersion of the Jewish people will end as God restores them to their land in Israel once more.
3. When that finally is accomplished, Israel will dwell in safety and be the people of God and God will be their exclusive God.
4. God will change Israel's heart so that their heart will no longer be divided, rather it will be singly focused on the Lord.
5. God will replant Israel in her land once more.

4

The Future Resurrection and Reunification of the Nation

Ezekiel 37:1–28

"These bones are the whole nation of Israel."

Ezekiel 37:11

Even though the thirty-seventh chapter of Ezekiel is one of the great chapters of the Bible, all too frequently it is sadly neglected by interpreters, pastors, and Bible readers, and it therefore remains largely unknown to many. The reason for the avoidance of this chapter may be that some wish to give all the promises made to Israel entirely over to the church in New Testament times (an interpretive practice mentioned earlier known as replacement theology, or supersessionism). But the passage in Ezekiel is so clear about the fact that the "bones" in verse 11 are the "bones [of] . . . the whole house of Israel," as the prophet authoritatively declares. If the language applies to Israel, how could it be directly applied to the church as its primary meaning?

This passage is set in a context of a series of six prophecies given to Ezekiel on the night before the news reaches both him and the exiles in Babylon about the destruction of Jerusalem (Ezek. 33:21–22). This news, then, introduces chapters 33–39 of Ezekiel with six famous prophecies about the future. In an amazing way, each of the six

31

prophecies describes how God will deal with the land of Israel and the people of that land whom he will restore to that promised land. These six prophecies follow six themes:

1. In the first message, God explains why he has laid the land of Israel a total waste. It is due to Israel's sinful practices, even despite their persistent hearing of the word from God. Their constant refusal to put those words into practice has earned them judgment from God (Ezek. 33:23–33).
2. The second message is a word of condemnation against those who were called to be shepherds or teachers of Israel, but who had selfishly taken care of themselves, thereby robbing God's people of the care they needed. Thus, the Lord himself will act as the Good Shepherd who, as the Davidic Messiah, will care for his neglected, bruised, and lost flock (Ezek. 34:1–31).
3. In his third message, Ezekiel announces that God will take on Edom, and all similar nations, that had harbored hostility against his people Israel, and bring on them his judgment. While God will devastate Israel's enemies, he will bring Israel home again, repopulate their land, and make them more prosperous than they were before (Ezek. 35:1–36:15).
4. In the next message, God will cleanse the people of Israel, revive them by the Spirit of God, bring them up from their graves, and return them back into the land of Israel again (Ezek. 36:16–37:14).
5. In the fifth message, the people of Israel will no longer be divided into ten northern tribes and two southern tribes, but they will be reunited into a single nation as one unified kingdom, as it was in Solomon's day (Ezek. 37:15–28).
6. Finally, in the last and sixth message, God will fight for Israel precisely when the nations led by Gog-Magog come up to destroy Israel in a future day (Ezek. 38–39).

Messages four and five seem to be at the heart of these six messages. But the question that remained was how could any picture of hope be given to a people who persistently led a life of ungodliness and sin? The answer given here is that they must first be punished with the (Babylonian) exile for the way they had defiled the land with their sin (Ezek. 36:17–20). But that is not the end to the story, for they will graciously be regathered back in their land (36:22–24, 33–38), cleansed of their iniquities (36:25–33) and given a new heart and a new spirit (36:26–27). That central vision of God's restoration of the nation came in Ezekiel's vision of the valley of the dry bones and the symbolism of the joining of the two sticks into one.

The Resurrection and Reunification of the Nation of Israel

Text: Ezekiel 37:1–28

Title: "The Resurrection and Reunification of the Nation of Israel"

Focal Point: Verse 11, "Son of Man, these bones are the whole nation of Israel. They say, 'Our bones are dried up and our hope is gone; we are cut off.'"

Homiletical Keyword: Promises

Interrogative: What? (What are the promises that God has made about the resurrection and reunification of the nation of Israel?)

Teaching Aim: To show that God will fulfill his promise to Israel to return them to their land once again and that he will make them one nation under one king with only one God worshiped by all of them.

Outline

1. Envisioning the Future of Israel under the Spirit of God—37:1–2
2. Experiencing a Physical Restoration from God—37:3–10
3. Enjoying a Spiritual Rebirth of the Nation from God—37:11–14
4. Restoring a Previously Divided Nation—37:15–17
5. Granting a Covenant of Peace as Israel Is Made Holy—37:18–28

Exegetical Study

1. Envisioning the Future of Israel under the Spirit of God—37:1–2

As with many of the prophecies about the future, this one is set in the form of apocalyptic literature. This literature uses symbolic and visionary language to describe events that will come in the future. The events are first recorded as they are seen by the prophet in a vision. Then what usually follows is an explanation given by a divine interpreter. Also of importance is the fact that this type of vision comes to people who are under heavy oppression and who have little hope for the days that lie ahead.

Apocalyptic literature uses symbols. In the instance before us, this thirty-seventh chapter of Ezekiel uses the symbol of bones followed by the symbolic writing of the names of Judah and Ephraim on each of the sticks as the two sticks of wood are joined to make one unified stick. In this visual way, Ezekiel makes his message memorable by the use of these symbols.

Regularly, apocalyptic literature has a straightforward threefold form:

1. the announcement of the vision with the name of the recipient, and the geographical place where that vision is received,
2. the description of the contents of the vision, and
3. the divine interpretation of the vision.

In the case of Ezekiel 37, Ezekiel is brought into the valley, which may be the same valley mentioned earlier in Ezekiel when he is by the Kebar River. Since Ezekiel uses the article "the" with the word "valley" in chapter 37, it may certainly be a well-known valley in that day, or one known from the earlier reference in his book.

The chapter begins by noting that "the hand of the LORD was upon [Ezekiel]," a phrase used in the book of Ezekiel seven times (1:3; 3:14, 22; 8:1; 33:22; 37:1; and 40:1). It signals that the power of God is on the prophet for the work he is to accomplish.

The prophet is led by the "Spirit of the LORD" and "set [down]" in the middle of the valley that is "full of bones" (1). As the prophet is "led . . . back and forth among [the bones]" (2), he notes the large number of dried and bleached bones. He is then asked by the Spirit of God, "Son of man [a favorite title of address for Ezekiel in this book], can these bones live?" (3). That inquiry seems to be something like a rhetorical question, for the vitality that had once belonged to these bones has long since expired. So what is the Spirit of God getting at? Certainly the Spirit of God knows the answer to such questions, so why ask me? Ezekiel must have concluded. The answer to the Spirit's inquiry is seen later in the text.

2. Experiencing a Physical Restoration from God—37:3–10

Ezekiel declines to answer the question, for he responds kindly, "O Sovereign LORD, you alone know" (3). Since God is God, all things are possible with him, just as he knows all things (Gen. 18:14; Jer. 32:17). So the prophet neither rules out any possibilities, nor does he affirm any either. The answer is in the hands of God. He knows if these bones can be made to live once again after they have been lying around the valley in the sun for so long.

Yahweh instructs the prophet to "prophesy to these bones and say to them, 'Dry bones, hear the word of the LORD!'" (4). Yahweh promises that with that declaration of his word, he will put "breath" into those dry bones and they will come back to life once again. The Lord himself will "attach tendons" to these same bones, put "flesh" on them, and "cover [them] with skin" (6a–c). It will be by this act that Israel will "know that [God was] . . . the LORD" (6d).

Amazingly, the prophet does not protest or ask how in the world such a thing could happen. Instead, he "prophesied as [he had been] commanded" (7a). He did not worry, as some might today, if preaching is all that relevant and reliable for situations such as he had not been faced with previously. In fact, the Hebrew syntax notes, "As [he] was prophesying, there was a noise, a rattling sound, and the bones came together" (7a–b). All of this came about as a result of the power of the word of God spoken by his messenger Ezekiel.

Nevertheless, despite the marvel of this assemblage, the bones were still inert and lifeless: "there was no breath in them" (8). The bones were without any vitality, but just sort of erect skeletons. Daniel Block remarks that the bones on the valley floor do not merely represent the victims of Nebuchadnezzar's war, who were left out in the fields, but "*they represent the entire house of Israel,* including even those who had been exiled by the Assyrians more than 130 years earlier."[1]

This prophecy is a two-staged prophetic act, which reminds many commentators of a similar double work of God in his double-staged act in creation. In that instance, he first formed man out of the dust of the ground; then, in a second stage of his creative force, he breathed into his nostrils the breath of life, and Adam became alive (Gen. 2:7). In a similar manner, as a second stage of this act of resurrecting the bones, God commands Ezekiel to "prophesy to the breath; prophesy, son of man, and say to it, 'This is what the Sovereign LORD says: Come from the four winds, O breath, and breathe into these slain, that they may live'" (9). Accordingly, as the prophet did so, "they came to life and stood up on their feet—a vast army" (10). The only difference here is that the breath, in the case of Ezekiel, does not come directly from Yahweh, as it did in creation, but from the "four winds" (9), which normally indicates the four corners of the earth (cf. Isa. 43:5–6; Jer. 31:8). In this way, according to some, the two-stepped restoration of the bones could well refer to Israel returning to her land in the last days, perhaps in an unconverted state—without life and vitality in spiritual things. But this interpretation must be weighed against the interpretation given by our Lord himself in verses 11–14.

3. Enjoying a Spiritual Rebirth of the Nation from God—37:11–14

As with other apocalyptic literature, any interpretation of this passage should closely follow the divine declaration given in the passage. Because of this, we must resist the temptation to make every detail mean some separate identity or have a formal reference, instead of following the major import of the vision. Therefore, verse 11 is the central focal point as it identifies the bones as being nothing less than "the whole house of Israel." The "bones" mean the same thing as the "slain" in verse 9.

The bones have three distinguishing marks:

1. They were "dried up" (11b), which points to the condition of the people of Israel who had by now been dead for a very long time.
2. Moreover, from the perspective of the persons represented by the bones, their "hope [was] gone" (11c).
3. The bones were "cut off" (11d), i.e., the individuals these bones represent were separated and dispersed from one another.

However, despite these disparaging conditions, once again the Lord commands the prophet to prophesy and relate what Yahweh himself had to say to the regathered and reassembled bones: "O my people, I am going to open your graves and bring you up from them; I will bring you back to the land of Israel" (12). Just when the condition of the people of Israel seemed lost (for their bones were dead and cut off [from God and from each other, or, so it seems], God says he will intervene as he "opens" their graves and "brings them back" into the land of Israel. Peter Craigie clearly affirms that the meaning of the text is such that "the prophecy, in other words, is not concerned with any theology of [a general] resurrection from the dead . . . ; rather, its focus is on the restoration of moribund exiles [of Israel] to new life in their original homeland."[2]

4. Restoring a Previously Divided Nation—37:15–17

In a new vision, which may have been a sequel to the vision of the dry bones in 37:1–14, Ezekiel is told by the Lord to perform another symbolic action. Just as ministers today use multisensory media to get their messages across to audiences, so the prophets often use symbolic actions for the same reason. Ezekiel is told by the word of the Lord to take two sticks of wood and to write on one: "Belonging to Judah and the Israelites associated with him," and on the other: "Ephraim's stick, belonging to Joseph and all the house of Israel associated with him" (16). The first stick includes Benjamin and Judah and the second includes the ten northern tribes, here represented by the house of Joseph. After he has inscribed each of the two sticks, he is to "join them together into one stick so that they will become one in [his] hand" (17). The united Jewish people of God would fulfill the promise God gave to Abraham in Genesis 12:1–3, 7 (cf. Ezek. 37:25). So central is this unification of the nation that the word "one" appears in Hebrew of this text nine times. This action will last forever, a fact also repeated five times in this same Hebrew text for emphasis. Add to all of that the expression "never again" will they be "two nations or be divided into two kingdoms" (22). Here is a declaration that had never been true of these two nations since the days shortly after King Solomon died in 931 BC. Surely this had to be a new act of God in the future, for nothing in history from 930 BC until Ezekiel's time could have fulfilled these words except a brand new act of reunification of the previously divided nation.

5. Granting a Covenant of Peace as Israel Is Made Holy—37:18–28

The Lord anticipates that the people will ask, "Won't you tell us what you mean by this?" (18). The prophet is to say to them that God will take these two sticks—symbolic of what had been, up until then, the long-termed division between the nation of Israel (the ten northern tribes) and the nation of Judah (the two southern tribes)—so that they will once more become "one," as they had been in the days of David and Solomon. Moreover, Yahweh will "take the Israelites out of the nations where they have gone," and he will "gather them from all around and bring them back into their own land" (21). Not only will they then be "one nation in the land" (22a), but Yahweh will set over them "one king" (22b). Once more, Yahweh says, "they will

be my people, and I will be their God" (22c). This will fulfill what
had been promised to Abraham in the famous Abrahamic covenant
(Gen. 12:1–3, 7; 16:10; 17:7–9; 22:17–18; 28:4, 13–15). "Never again"
will these two nations be divided (Ezek. 37:22c) or referred to as two
separate nations, promises the Lord. The united people will forever be
cleansed of their old idolatry and their penchant for sinning against
the commandments of God.

When God restores Israel to her land once more in the last days,
he will enact "a covenant of peace" (Ezek. 34:25–29; 37:26). Under
this covenant, Israel will be restored to her land; she will see a real
increase in her numbers (Gen. 22:17–18), and the Lord will place his
sanctuary in her midst forever (Ezek. 37:26–27; 40:5–43:9). No other
nation will be able to say that the Lord himself dwells with it in his
own sanctuary as he dwells in the land of Israel (Ezek. 37:28; Ezek.
40–48), for what God will do here is unique in all the world. Here
in the land, Israel will for the first time in her history dwell in peace
forever from then on under the rule of her king, the Messiah Jesus of
Nazareth (34:25–29; 37:26; cf. 38:11).

Conclusions

1. Despite Israel's continual rejection of her Lord, God will extend
   his mercy and grace as he brings the dead bones of the nation
   together once again with his life and *breathes into them* so they
   can live as a nation once again.
2. This will be the result of the work of the Holy Spirit upon the
   nation of Israel, subsequently bringing them to repentance and
   faith in the Messiah, Jesus of Nazareth, in the last days.
3. Instead of remaining two separate nations, divided since the
   days when Solomon's reign ended, God will reunite the southern
   two tribes with the northern ten tribes into one whole—never
   to be divided for all of time and eternity!
4. Over this reunified single nation God himself will rule as king
   and shepherd over his people.
5. God will place his sanctuary in the midst of his people as he
   once more becomes their God and they become his people.

5

The Future Return of Israel to the Land of Promise

Zechariah 10:2-12

"I will bring them back . . . and there will not be enough
room for them."

Zechariah 10:10

Beside the promise of the first and second coming of Messiah,
few promises of the Old Testament are as intricately interwoven
throughout the entire Scriptures as the promise of the land of Israel
to Abraham and his descendants. Not only would the promise-plan of
God be without a concrete anchor in reality without the people and
land of Israel, but the promise made to the church would be without
any firm attachment to any past history and to what God had planned
to provide for all who believed. If the church had not been rooted in
the concrete promises of the calling of a nation and the gift of the
land, it too would float in the air without any grounding in the past.

Many public readers of the Bible tend to get confused when they
read the history of Israel, for the Jewish people were scattered and
separated from their land on three separate occasions, and on three
more separate times they were (or will be) returned back to that
same piece of real estate by the grace and mercy of God. Therefore,

39

one must carefully compare each of the prophecies of scattering and returning with the actual claims of Scripture.

One of the centerpieces in the promise-plan of God is the prediction Yahweh made with Abraham and his descendants to give them the land that sits at the juncture of three major portions of the earth's populations: Africa, Europe, and Asia. There, both in the fullness of time and in the fullness of geography, God placed Israel on this significant land-bridge between the continents and the nations. What began in Genesis 12:7 ("The LORD appeared to Abram and said, 'To your offspring I will give this land'"), continued in Genesis 15:18–21 ("On that day the LORD made a covenant with Abram and said, 'To your descendants I give this land, from the river of Egypt [i.e., the Wadi Mitzraim] to the great river, the Euphrates—the land of the Kenites, Kenizzites, Kadmonites, Hittites, Perizzites, Rephaites, Amorites, Canaanites, Girgashites and Jebusites'"). Accordingly, this was not some ethereal, nonmaterial gift, or some type of a spiritual blessing, but it was a specific piece of property located in real geography.

Genesis 15:18–21 confirmed this promise by further describing which land God had meant when he uttered this promise. But it was Genesis 17:7–8 that locked it in as an "everlasting covenant." There God promised:

> I will establish my covenant as an everlasting covenant between me and you and your descendants after you for the generations to come, to be your God and the God of your descendants after you. The whole land of Canaan, where you are now an alien, I will give as an everlasting possession to you and your descendants after you; and I will be their God.

Thus it happened that God promised in perpetuity to Abraham, and his descendants after him, the land that stretched from the little Wadi Mitzraim across the Sinai in the south all the way to the Euphrates River in the east, including Lebanon and large portions of Syria. There were no exclusions of the West Bank, or of the Gaza Strip, as is the reality of today's present geographical arrangement.

Abram, renamed Abraham in Genesis 17, never actually took possession of this land, but all of this would be fulfilled at a later date. In the meantime, one of Jacob's sons, Joseph, had been sold by his own brothers into the land of Egypt. However, Joseph was subsequently raised to second in command of the land of Egypt, saving Egypt, as well as his own family, from the ill effects of the seven-year famine. As a result of his position, he was able to invite his whole family of some seventy persons to come to Egypt, and thus the family of Abraham later grew from seventy persons to a nation of several million by the time they left Egypt some four hundred years later.

The First Return of the Jewish People

As the years went on, a change in the Egyptian government forced the alien population of these Jewish people into slavery until God raised up Moses as his instrument of deliverance for the nation. Thus, the book of Exodus records the first return to the land, even though this return was marred by forty years of wandering in the wilderness. However, as Joshua took over after the death of Moses, God repeated the promise of the land to Joshua. Joshua was to cross over the Jordan to Canaan as he went "into the land I am about to give [you]—to [all the] Israelites" (Josh. 1:2). Moreover, God once again gave a specific geographical description of that land: "Your territory will extend from the desert [in the south] to Lebanon [in the north], and from the great River, the Euphrates—all the Hittite country—to the Great Sea on the west [the Mediterranean]" (Josh. 1:4).

Even though the people of Israel had been warned that unless they obeyed the Lord they would once again be driven out of the land, Israel failed, and the worst happened to them. From the halcyon days of kings David and Solomon, Israel—now divided into the northern ten tribes, called Ephraim after the name of the largest tribe, and the two southern tribes of Judah and Benjamin—quickly lapsed into the worship of pagan gods and goddesses and awful moral decline. This would spell their defeat and expulsion from the land.

The Second Departure from the Land

In the eighth century the Assyrians swept the ten northern tribes into captivity in 721/722 BC. Not too long after that, the southern two tribes were also expelled from the land, only this time it was to the conqueror Nebuchadnezzar of Babylon in 586 BC. Now some of the people were scattered all over northern Mesopotamia by the Assyrians, and the others were scattered later all over southern Mesopotamia, which became known in that day as the "Babylonian captivity." What had been predicted had happened: the nation, both north and south, had been expelled from the land and scattered.

The Second Return to the Land

But God had not forgotten his promise to the Jewish people, despite their insistence on disregarding and disobeying him. Through the prophet Jeremiah, the Lord said: "When seventy years are completed for Babylon, I will come to you and fulfill my gracious promise to bring you back to this place" (Jer. 29:10).

Almost seventy years later, the prophet Daniel, now around eighty years of age, read Jeremiah's prophecy about the seventy-year captivity (Dan. 9:2). If God had spoken such a promise, Daniel prayed that God would then be pleased not to delay their return to the land, but to carry out what he had said he would do now that the seventy years were coming to an end.

Jeremiah's words and Daniel's prayers were answered, as the book of Ezra recorded, when nearly fifty thousand Jewish exiles from Babylon returned home in 536 BC, and after a twenty-year struggle internally, they rebuilt the (second) temple in 516 BC in Jerusalem. Nehemiah contributed to this by leading in the rebuilding of the walls of Jerusalem in 445 BC.

Later, in 20 BC, the Roman government, acting to favor Israel, reconstructed the second temple that had been rebuilt in 516 BC, work which was finally completed in AD 64, built of stones that had come from underneath the city of Jerusalem. Once again, Israel seemed secure!

The Third Departure

The glory of that temple rebuilt by Herod was short lived, for by AD 70 Jerusalem was destroyed by the Romans, the temple was consumed in flames, and hundreds of thousands of pilgrims present in the city of Jerusalem for the feast days were slaughtered by the Romans. With this conquest, Israel once again lost control of the promised land. Jesus had predicted that this magnificent temple would be destroyed so that one stone would not be left on another (Matt. 24:2). But just as tragic, if not more so, was what would happen in the centuries that followed.

Afflicted by one persecution after another, the Jewish people were driven from their land by both pagans and Christians alike. Israel seemed to be cut off from the promised land forever. In the eighth century AD, the Arabs took possession of this ancient land, only to be harassed by the Christian crusaders, who set up a presence in the twelfth century. But the Christian crusaders were also defeated fairly quickly by Saladin in AD 1187, and the Ottoman Turks took over in 1517 and held on to the land until Turkey was defeated in World War I. In 1917, General Allenby of Great Britain conquered Jerusalem, and then the British occupied the land of Israel.

The Beginnings of the Third Return

Never had the thoughts of any Jewish return to the land been without problems, even though as early as AD 1871 some Jews had started a trickle of returnees. By 1881 there were about twenty-five thousand Jews settled in the land, but no formal declarations or permissions had been announced. However, in 1897 Theodore Herzl announced the goal of reclaiming the land as a home for the Jews at the first Zionist Congress. But it was not until November 2, 1917, that the British foreign secretary, Arthur J. Balfour, issued what became known as the "Balfour Declaration." In this declaration, Britain announced its approval of Israel's goal to establish a nation with these words: "His Majesty's Government view with favour the establishment in Palestine of a national home for the Jewish people. . . ."

Opposition from the Arab world was intense, and Britain's attempt to please both the Jewish and the Arab people at the same time prevented any real progress toward the announced goal up until the time of World War II, which broke out in 1939 and continued until 1945.

However, on May 14, 1948, after World War II, British rule in Palestine ended, and on May 15, 1948, the United Nations, supported by the United States and Russia (then the USSR), gave a directive that a Jewish state, of some five thousand square miles, was to be formed along with an Arab state. At that time, Israel's population consisted of sixty-five thousand Jewish people and hundreds of thousands of Arabs.

Now more than sixty years later, it would appear that this was the beginning of the third return of the Jewish people, only this time they would come literally from all over the world. A period of initial tranquility in Israel proved to be no more than a false peace; an international betrayal and armed opposition from several sources would ensue, known as the "time of trouble for Jacob" (Jer. 30:7).

However, the full return will not be completed until the period of time surrounding the events associated with the second coming of our Lord and his return back to earth. In the meantime, one attack on Israel after another occurred, beginning in October 1956, as the Israeli army overran the Gaza Strip, and was advancing well on their way into Egypt, when the major powers halted Israel. This was followed by the Six-Day War in June 1967. In a preemptive strike, Israeli jets flew in low over the Mediterranean Sea and over Egypt, flying in from the north and northwest and destroying the Egyptian air force, while Israeli torpedo boats and commandos demolished most of Egypt's naval power. By now Israel had increased her territory to some thirty-four thousand square miles and doubled her population. This was followed by the Yom Kippur War starting on October 6, 1973. As the call for a cease-fire went out, twenty thousand Egyptian soldiers were pinned down east of the Suez Canal by the Israeli army, but were rescued once again by the cease-fire.

In an attempt to ease Israeli-Egyptian relations, Anwar Sadat, president of Egypt, was invited to address the Knesset in Jerusalem, as he met with Menachem Begin, the prime minister of Israel. In September of 1978, the President of the United States, Jimmy Carter, met Prime Minister Begin and President Sadat in the United States and issued what became known as the Camp David Accords, which resulted in a peace accord between Egypt and Israel.

Widespread random acts of terrorism against Israel continued, however, in the 1990s and on into the twenty-first century. Nevertheless, Israel has miraculously survived, despite the enormity of the modern weapons poised against her and the armies that have been advanced against her from time to time. Moreover, her population has increased to some seven million with a million to a million-and-a-half Russian Jews immigrating to Israel along with a large number of Ethiopian Jews also. Both of these Jewish groups have been most responsive to the gospel message.

It is in light of these events that we turn to a key prophecy that featured the future third return to her land from all over the world in Zechariah 10 in a time significantly after the Jewish people had returned from the Babylonian exile. Thus, this return could not be confused with the second return of the Jewish people to Israel from the Babylonian captivity.

The Third Return of Israel to the Land of Promise

Text: Zechariah 10:2–12

Title: "The Third Return of Israel to the Land of Promise"

Focal Point: Verses 9–10, "Though I scatter them among the peoples, yet in distant lands they will remember me. . . . I will bring them back from Egypt and gather them from Assyria. I will bring them to Gilead and Lebanon, and there will not be room enough for them."

Homiletical Keyword: Contrasts

Interrogative: What? (What are the contrasts between the corrupted leaders or false shepherds and the good leaders and true shepherds of the people?)

Teaching Aim: To show how Israel has suffered not only for her own sin, but from the corrupted leadership she has had in deference to the compassionate leadership God plans to give her in the last days as he brings Israel back to the land of his promise for the third time.

Outline

1. God Is Angered by Israel's Corrupted Leadership—10:2–3
2. God's Model for a New Leadership Is His Messiah—10:4–5
3. God Will Regather Israel Once More in Her Land—10:6–12

Exegetical Study

1. God Is Angered by Israel's Corrupted Leadership—10:2–3

The prophet Zechariah introduces the new metaphor of the "shepherd" as another word for a "leader." The term "shepherd" was used in the ancient Near East to designate a number of positions, each with leadership responsibility: teachers, prophets, priests, judges, rulers, kings, and governors. However, in the days of Zechariah, the leaders had abused their positions of service and turned them into positions of privilege and as opportunities for abuse of the public.

Acting more like sheep, the people were sitting prey for these ruthless rulers. The people were powerless, in most instances, to even begin a rescue of themselves. As a result, the anger of God burned against these corrupt leaders, and he threatened to punish them. They were abusing God's flock. Therefore, God would "make them [his people] like a proud horse." This expression signaled the fact that God would turn his bullied sheep into royal horses that excelled in battle. They would act like war horses and overthrow their oppressive leaders.

Another place where the corrupt leaders had gone wrong was in the direction from which they were getting their guidance. They put their trust in their "idols," or "teraphim" (= household idols) (2a), and in their "diviners" who claimed to see "visions" (2b). But worse still was the fact that they taught their people to put their trust as well in these same idols and diviners.

But the dreams of these diviners were simply "false" (2c). "[T]hey [gave] comfort in vain" (2d) to the people, who struggled to gain a much more accurate direction for life and living from their leaders. God did speak on occasion through dreams, but these charlatans could not claim the same source or authority. The prophet Jeremiah had castigated such fraudulent divination in no uncertain terms in Jeremiah 23:32 and 27:9–10. Instead of going to God himself, these false and corrupt religionists inspected the entrails of birds and animals to determine what was the proper course of action (Josh. 13:22; 1 Sam. 6:2). It was an outright denial of the providence and will of God.

As a result, the leadership was terribly misguided, and they left the people of Israel to "wander like sheep" (2e). When sheep begin to wander, it is a clear sign that the trouble is that the sheep "lack[ed] a shepherd" (2f). Therefore, with unreliable and corrupt leadership, the people were in effect leaderless. They had no real shepherd, or anyone who cared for them, or who even knew what to do.

No wonder God's anger burned against these false and incompetent shepherds (3). He must punish such fraudulent shepherds; he could not let these leaders get away with what they had inflicted on his flock, for God himself will not abandon his own flock. The contrast in leaders could not be greater!

2. God's Model for a New Leadership Is His Messiah—10:4–5

God will give a new, stable leadership that will arise directly "from Judah" (4). This new leader will be such a contrast from those corrupt leaders that the difference could not be more clearly set forth. It will not be another mere mortal, but it will be the One who will be known as "the cornerstone," "the tent peg," the "battle bow," and the "ruler" par excellence. This leader will arise out of Judah, as Genesis 49:10 had promised, but he will be known by other names as well. The Messiah will also be called the "cornerstone" or "capstone" in Psalm 118:22. As such, this title refers to the steadfastness and reliability of the same One who in another passage (Jer. 30:21) is referred to as the "ruler."

The "tent peg" originally depicted either the hook in the center of the tent, where all the frequently used items of the household were kept, or the peg in the ground that secured the tent and kept it taut. The reference here is probably to the hook, since the same imagery is used in Isaiah 22:23 to refer to Eliakim, the son of Hilkiah, who also had a leadership position. There too the imagery refers at once to Eliakim and to the coming Messiah, who will be the leader in the house of Judah, and to whom "the key to the house of David" will be given.

The "battle bow" serves as a symbol of strength for military conquest (2 Kings 13:17). This brand new type of leader, in contrast to what Judah had had to put up with until then, will be ready to take up the cause of the promise-plan of God. He will be the One who will sit on the white horse of Revelation 6:2, and who will hold a "bow" as he "[rides] out as a conqueror bent on conquest."

Using the concept of synecdoche (wherein the part is put for the whole), the idea of Zechariah 10:5 seems to be that God will empower all his people to overthrow all false leaders and oppressors. Thus, "together they will be like mighty men trampling the muddy streets in battle . . . [b]ecause the LORD is with them" (5). So expert will these revived people be that they will handily defeat and embarrass each foe or opponent that comes against them.

3. God Will Regather Israel Once More in Her Land—10:6–12

God here promises to "strengthen" and to "save" both the southern "house of Judah" and the northern "house of Joseph," which of course point to the two southern tribes and the ten northern tribes that have been separated since 931 BC at the end of Solomon's rule! God will now "restore[/bring back]" both of these houses, formerly in the divided kingdom, because he will show "compassion[/mercy]" (6) on them.

Since this prediction was made some time after December 7, 518 BC (Zech. 7:1), almost twenty years after Judah's return from the

Babylonian exile, this cannot be a promise of that second return, but a promise of a third return, which was yet to come beyond Zechariah's day. Moreover, this return will not be from Babylon alone, but God specifically promises that he will "bring them back from Egypt and gather them from Assyria" (10). They will come from all the "distant lands" (9), and it will involve not just Judah, who went into Babylon, but also "the house of Joseph" that went into the Assyrian captivity in 721/722 BC. The so-called "ten lost tribes" will not be "lost" any longer, so long as God maintains the ancient promise he had given to Abraham, Isaac, and Jacob, as well as the one he had given to David.

God promises that he will "answer" both houses of Israel (6) and "redeem them," so that they will "be as numerous as before" (8). The northern tribes—here referred to as the "Ephraimites," designating the largest Joseph clan that stood for all of the ten northern tribes—will be transformed into acting "like mighty men" (7a). No wonder there is "rejoic[ing] in the LORD" (7c–d).

Just as flocks will hear their shepherd "whistling[/signaling]" for them (Judg. 5:16), so the Lord will "signal[/whistle] [for his people] and gather them in" (8a–b) from all over the world. This return from the Diaspora around the world will end the time of Israel's scattering and result in an increase in their numbers such as they had not seen theretofore (8d). Since the times of Israel's exile into Assyria and Babylon, God had withheld his blessings by and large, but this new increase will be another indication that the former days have passed and a new day has arrived for Israel.

Even though the Lord is the One who will make all of this possible, the people must also "remember" their Lord (9b) while they are still in those distant countries. Surely this is exactly what Moses had taught the Israelites back in Leviticus 26:40–42: "But if they will confess their sins and the sins of their fathers—. . . which made me hostile toward them so that I sent them into the land of their enemies—then when their uncircumcised hearts are humbled and they pay for their sin, I will remember my covenant with Jacob and my covenant with Isaac and my covenant with Abraham and I will remember the land." Then it will be possible for Israel to return to her land and for "[them] and their children [to] survive" (9c).

God will bring Israel back to "Gilead and Lebanon" (10), which are part of the greatly expanded boundaries of Israel given earlier in the promise-plan of God. Gilead is the area we refer to today as the "Golan Heights," which extends northeast from the Sea of Galilee over to the Euphrates River through the Damascus corridor. Lebanon is the nation to the north of Israel along the Mediterranean coast embracing the cities of Tyre, Sidon, Beirut, and Byblos. However, even with this expanded territory, all space in Israel will be quickly used up as the flood of returnees leaves no space left for more immigrants.

The Lord himself will go ahead of Israel to remove all the barriers for their return, just as he opened up the Red Sea (11; Exod. 14:21–31) and the Jordan River (Josh. 3:14–17). Even though this text refers to the Nile River in verse 11, it probably refers here figuratively to the Euphrates River, which the Lord will also cause to dry up in that day so the returnees can walk across easily (Isa. 11:15).

Such talk of a third return of Israel to her land may seem to some as a lot of bravado talk, or the height of chutzpah (a Yiddish word for unmitigated effrontery or impudence). But verse 12 affirms that all this will be accomplished by the power of God, who will "strengthen them in the LORD," so that "in his name they will walk" (12). This same figure of walking in the name of the Lord is used in Micah 4:5 of the lifestyle of those who are in Messiah's kingdom, thus it speaks of a time when the benefits of the new covenant will be fully realized at the time of the second coming of our Lord.

Conclusions

1. The contrasts between the ruthless, oppressive shepherds of the past and the coming Good Shepherd could not be more dramatic.
2. The Good Shepherd who will come will be Israel's "cornerstone," their "tent peg," and their "battle bow," just as he is our Messiah as well.
3. This is one of the most important passages of some two to three dozen major texts in the Old Testament that speak of a return of the nation Israel back to her land the third time.

Part 3

The New Davidic King and the City of the Great King in the Old Testament

With out the second coming of Messiah, all teaching about events that are to come in the future would lack their real epicenter. Our Lord is the center and the heart of all that is to take place in eschatology. An eschatology without a Christology is like a book without a first and final chapter, for Jesus is the *alpha* and *omega* to all history and eschatology!

More often than not, however, interpreters of the Old Testament predictions about Messiah or the end-times events wait until they have found a New Testament basis for proceeding prior to attempting any exegesis of the ancient Word of God. However, our Lord meant that those living in those earlier days should have understood the words of the Old Testament and had an adequate appreciation of his first coming, not to mention his second advent. That is why our Lord took Cleopas and that other unnamed disciple to task for their lack of understanding of the events of the Lord's death, burial, and resurrection (Luke 24:25–27; cf. Matt. 13:17) on that first Easter as they walked to Emmaus.

Therefore, if these two disciples could have understood the events that the Old Testament predicted concerning Jesus's first advent, even before the New Testament was written, should anything less be said to us in our day about what the Old Testament predicted about the second advent—with or without the New Testament?

Some will likewise object that it is only the New Testament that gives us the teaching that there are two comings of our Lord. For example, in Jewish interpretation of the Tanak (= Old Testament), it is claimed that Messiah will not come until there is a time of peace, so that could only mean a single coming! This is what a Jewish rabbi claimed in a televised debate I had with him over the topic, "Is Jesus the Messiah?" I responded, however, that the Old Testament did teach the same two comings of Messiah, for the prophet Zechariah taught, "They will look on me, the one they have pierced, and they will mourn for him as one mourns for an only child" (12:10). I asked, "Isn't this context one that speaks of Messiah also coming in a time of peace?" He agreed that it did teach Messiah would come in a time of peace.

Then I asked my rabbi friend Dr. Pinchas Lapide, "Who is speaking in this text?" He replied, "The Almighty." "Good," I said. Then how did the Almighty get "pierced"? He replied, he did not know. I responded, "I have an idea—it was on the cross!" This was in Messiah's first coming, yet the text goes on to talk about the fact that he will also come and establish peace on the earth in another coming to earth.

Closely associated with the promise of the two comings of the Messiah is the repeated reference to Zion and the central role Jerusalem will play in that future day of our Lord. No wonder the psalmist sings in Psalm 48:1–2, "Great is the LORD, and most worthy of praise, in the city of our God, his holy mountain. It is beautiful in its loftiness; the joy of the whole earth . . . is Mount Zion, the city of the Great King." So it will be even more so in that day when our Lord returns and Jerusalem is set up as the teaching and worship center for the whole earth.

6

The Branch of the Lord
and the New Zion

Isaiah 2:2–5; 4:2–6

"Come, let us go up to the mountain of the Lord."

Isaiah 2:3

Donald E. Gowan, in his book *Eschatology in the Old Testament*, announces that "Jerusalem appears with a prominence unparalleled by any other ['last things'] theme. It was surprising to find [this] 'center' [in] OT eschatology" (bracketed insertions mine).[1] It is therefore astonishing that the hopes that Israel had for itself and for the world focused on one city, Jerusalem, also known as Zion. However, it is the presence of the Messiah that makes this judgment possible, for without him Zion still would be just like any other major city in the world.

In his study of Old Testament eschatology, Gowan suggests that one good place to start to examine this theme of Jerusalem is Zechariah 8.[2] After Zechariah first answers traditional questions about the true nature and value of worship in chapter 7 for the Jewish people who had returned from Babylonian captivity and rebuilt the temple, he then turns to talk about the future of Zion (mentioned twice, in 8:1, 2) and Jerusalem (mentioned six times, 8:3 [twice], 4, 8, 15, 22).

Zechariah 8 carries some of the main elements contained in this major theme of Jerusalem as the center of Old Testament eschatology:

1. God will bring Israel back from the east and west to live in Jerusalem (8:7–8) once again.
2. The nations will no longer mock and despise Israel (8:13).
3. Jerusalem will be the dwelling place of the Lord, the City of Truth (8:3).
4. The nations will voluntarily come to Zion to entreat the Lord's favor and to seek him (8:20–23).
5. The future inhabitants of Jerusalem will speak the truth and obey the torah (8:16–17).
6. Jerusalem's streets will be filled with children playing and men and women who have lived to a ripe old age (8:4–5).
7. God will reverse the curse on nature as the vine and the fields produce and the heavens send down their dew (8:12).

Jerusalem has been the center for the worship of Yahweh ever since Abraham was asked by God to sacrifice his son on Mount Moriah (Gen. 22:2), which later in Scriptures is clearly identified with Jerusalem (2 Chron. 3:1). Years afterward, King David brought the ark of the covenant into Zion (2 Sam. 6), so that from that time forward, Jerusalem was the place to worship God, for the Lord had chosen Zion to be his resting place (Ps. 132:13–14). Henceforth, Zion has been lifted up as the place where the worship of God could best be accomplished (e.g., Pss. 46, 48, 76).

Not only do the Psalms celebrate Zion as the proper place to worship God, and where he has designated his resting place, but so do the prophets. They point to Zion of the future as a major teaching locale and central place to celebrate the worship of the Living God. For example, Zion figures prominently in Micah 4, Daniel 9:2, 24–26, some thirty-three times in the prophet Isaiah, ten times in Ezekiel, thirteen times in Jeremiah, eight in Zechariah, Zephaniah 3:14–20, Joel 3:17–21, Obadiah 15–21, Haggai 2:9, and Malachi 3:4.[3]

All in all, it is declared that this little hill of Mount Zion (now about 2,500 feet above sea level), which is not even as tall as the Mount of Olives at the present time, will be the highest mountain on earth! Whether this is a topographical statement or more of a theological statement is not immediately possible to determine. But it certainly points to the fact that special prominence will be given to this mountain, which will be a world mountain in the estimation of all in the future, when the Lord himself takes up residence there!

Two passages are especially prominent in portraying the role Zion will play in the future: Isaiah 2:2–5 and 4:2–6. It is to these two passages that we turn for a greater perspective on what difference the Lord himself will make to this piece of real estate at the eastern end of the Mediterranean Sea.

The Branch of the Lord and the New Zion

Texts: Isaiah 2:2–5; 4:2–6

Title: "The Branch of the Lord and the New Zion"

Focal Points: Isaiah 2:3, "Come, let us go up to the mountain of the LORD, to the house of the God of Jacob. He will teach us his ways, so that we may walk in his paths"; Isaiah 4:5, "The LORD will create over all of Mount Zion and over those who assemble there a cloud of smoke by day and a glow of flaming fire by night; over all the glory will be a canopy."

Homiletical Keyword: Basis

Interrogative: What? (What are the bases for such strong expressions of hope as Messiah takes up his residence in the new Zion?)

Teaching Aim: To show how all the nations of the world will annually go up to Jerusalem to meet the Lord and to be personally instructed by him.

Outline

1. Jerusalem Will Be the Worldwide Center of Messiah's Teaching and Peace—2:2–5
    1.1. Zion, the City of Worldwide Travel—2:2
    1.2. Zion, the City of Worldwide Teaching—2:3
    1.3. Zion, the City of Worldwide Peace—2:4
    1.4. Zion, the City of Worldwide Invitation—2:5
2. Jerusalem Will Be the Residence of the Branch of the Lord—4:2–6

Exegetical Study

1. Jerusalem Will Be the Worldwide Center of Messiah's Teaching and Peace—2:2–5

Isaiah 2:2–5 appears almost in verbatim form in Micah 4:1–4. But it is impossible to say which form was the original, for both prophets lived and ministered in the eighth century BC. However, the fact that this same teaching appears twice seems to indicate not only its popularity in that day, but also signals its importance in the role it would play.

1.1. Zion, the City of Worldwide Travel—2:2

The setting for the announcements that are to be made here is once again "in the last days" (2:2a), an expression that refers to those "future days" when Messiah will appear for the second time on earth. But the New Testament later reveals that these "last days" begin with the first coming of Christ, as Acts 2:17 and Hebrews 1:2 demonstrate. Thus, there was and is both a "now" aspect to these "last days" and a "not yet" aspect that awaits the events connected with the Lord's second advent. This phenomenon, which scholars refer to as "inaugurated eschatology," can be seen in texts such as 1 John 3:2, which teaches, "Dear friends, *now* we are the children of God, and what we will be has *not yet* been made known" (emphasis mine). So there is both a "now" and a "not yet" aspect to those "last days." Hebrews also teaches in 1:1–2 that "in the past God spoke to our forefathers through the prophets at many times and in various ways, but *in these last days* he has spoken unto us by his Son" (emphasis mine). According to this statement, the first coming of our Lord opened up parts of those "last days" that are to come.

However, in this passage in Isaiah 2:2–5, the events described here await their fulfillment at the second advent of our Lord Jesus. At that time, God will judge the nations and finally worldwide peace will ensue as Jerusalem becomes the governing center in the world.

At that coming time, Isaiah teaches that God will establish "the mountain of the Lord's temple . . . as chief among the mountains" (2b–c). The reason this mountain will be the destination of choice for all the world in that day is that Jews and gentiles will come to Jerusalem's "holy mountain" to worship and to be instructed by the Lord in the time when the Lord returns back to earth once again (Isa. 11:9; 27:13; 57:13; 65:11, 25; 66:20). Thus, the nations of the earth will gather in Jerusalem for learning and worshiping at the feet of the best of all teachers, the Lord himself!

Moreover, the city of Zion will be elevated (2d–e). The prophet Zechariah describes how the Mount of Olives will be split in two, with one half moving north and the other half moving south, apparently in a mighty earthquake, as the Lord touches down on the Mount of Olives, which is to the east of Jerusalem (Zech. 14:4). A valley between the two separated parts of the Mount of Olives will form an escape route for those who flee from the city of Jerusalem in that day, when the Lord will go out and fight against the nations. Moreover, the whole land, from Geba, which is six miles northeast of Zion, to Rimmon, thirty-two miles south of Jerusalem, will be raised up and become level like the Arabah (Zech. 14:10). So the uplifting mentioned here may be more than a metaphorical expression of the city's being raised above the hills. It also may well be a topographical change of enormous proportions, making it ready for the huge influx of travelers from all over the globe. Thus, the temple site and its city will be exalted not only in terms of its spiritual esteem, by virtue of the divine instruction from the God of Israel, but it will simultaneously be a physical reality as well.

So heavy will the traffic toward Jerusalem be that the large numbers of arrivals will appear to be much like a stream of water over the landscape (2e) when observed from a distant perspective. The nations will make their pilgrimage to Zion to see and hear from their Lord.

1.2. Zion, the City of Worldwide Teaching—2:3

The desire of the nations, as expressed voluntarily on their part, will be to go to Jerusalem. It appears that all former barriers, such as race, gender, social structure, educational levels, or denominations will be transcended, as the nations come by mutual consent and by mutual urging of one another ("Come, let us go"; 3b). What these people want is to be taught God's ways, so that they can walk in his paths (3d–e). Through their grasping the truth of God's "ways" (3d), their own lives are redirected to live in accordance with that truth. What a remarkable change from the former days, when the "ways" of God generally were not sought, highly regarded, or obeyed by those who heard these same words from the lips of the prophets.

Just as God will teach "his ways" (3d) in that coming day, so his "law" will simultaneously go out from Zion (3f), and his "word" will go out from Jerusalem (3g). The "house of . . . Jacob" (3c) will take on a role it had never realized previously in history.

1.3. ZION, THE CITY OF WORLDWIDE PEACE—2:4

There will be no need for an International Court of Justice, such as the one in the Hague (Netherlands), or for a Supreme Court in the land, for the Lord himself "will judge between the nations and will settle disputes for many peoples" (4a–b). This means an end to all prolonged disputes over territories, tariffs, personal rights, mineral rights, and arguments of that sort. The world's most fair and most just judge will be in charge, the Lord himself.

As a result of the new advocacy for justice from the Lord himself, one can just as well forget all about national armaments as well. Instead, those weapons of war will be turned into implements of agriculture (4c–d). In millennial Jerusalem, one can just plain forget about going to war against one another (4e–f). They can just as well forget about "tak[ing] up [their] sword[s] against [other] nation[s]" (4e), for those weapons of war are now made over into "plowshares" (4c). Likewise, they can drop any notion of picking up their "spears" (4d), for they too will already have been converted into "pruning hooks" (4d). Not only is the hardware of war no longer necessary, but there is no need to "train for war anymore" (4f). So one may say "goodbye" to the draft as well.

With the dominion of that old dragon, the serpent, removed, there can now be a return to the pleasures and joys of Eden. In that day the "in" implements will be "ploughshares" and "pruning hooks," not spears and swords.

1.4. ZION, THE CITY OF WORLDWIDE INVITATION—2:5

The word that comes spontaneously from the nations that gather in Zion on that day will be an invitation to "come, O house of Jacob, let us walk in the light of the LORD" (2:5). This is a 180-degree turnabout from the former days when "walk[ing] in the light of the LORD" was often the furthest thing from the heart and mind of the twelve tribes.

2. Jerusalem Will Be the Residence of the Branch of the Lord—4:2–6

Like two bookends, Isaiah 2:2–5 and Isaiah 4:2–6 form an inclusio, as if the promise of God's deliverance forms God's final answer, rather than the judgment section of Isaiah 2:6–4:1, which comes in between. Thus the section ends as it began, with the good news that the Lord is the one who will deliver the "survivors," a group mentioned frequently in Isaiah (e.g., in 4:2; 6:13; 7:3).

Once again, the setting is placed "in that day" (2a), as it was in Isaiah 2:2, "in the last days" (cf. 2:12, 17; 3:7, 18; 4:1). This is the period of the messianic era, which encompasses those events that belong to the time of the second advent of our Lord. That advent will follow the judging of Israel and the nations that have not obeyed or believed on the Lord.

The name "Branch of the LORD," however, is one of the technical terms used in the Old Testament prophets for the Messiah who is to return again (along with the parallel terms of the "shoot," or "twig," in Isaiah 11:1 and 53:2). The term "Branch" is a most interesting one, for it reveals four different aspects of Messiah in three separate prophetic books of the Old Testament. Just as a portrait painter would not combine in his one painting all the various offices a person held whom he wished to immortalize, so the Scriptures under the same title paint four different paintings in three different prophets, that each could thereby reveal four different characteristics of Messiah.

In Jeremiah 23:5–6 (repeated in Jer. 33:15), Messiah is called "*David*, a righteous Branch." This title certainly emphasizes Messiah's royal status and descent from the line of King David. In Zechariah 3:8, he is "my *servant*, the Branch." This title stresses the fact that Messiah will come not to be served, but to serve others and give his life as a ransom for many. In Zechariah 6:12–13, Messiah is named "the *man* whose name is Branch." This title emphasizes the fact that he will also be fully man as well as divine. The final text is the one in our passage, Isaiah 4:2, "the Branch of the LORD," which also focuses on the fact that Messiah will also be divine.

The early church fathers were accustomed to drawing four pictures of our Lord from these four "Branch" titles and associating these four with the four Gospels, as portrayed in Matthew, Mark, Luke, and John. Matthew portrays Messiah as one from the *kingly* line of David, as seen in the genealogy his Gospel begins with. Mark 10:45 states that the purpose of Branch's life and of Mark's Gospel is that "the Son of Man [another title for Messiah] did not come to be served, but to serve, and to give his life a ransom for many." Hence, Jesus is "my *servant*, the Branch." Luke emphasizes the fact that Messiah is fully man as did the title "the *man* whose name is

Branch." Finally, the Gospel of John points often to our Lord's *deity*, and the title "the Branch of the *Lord*" carries the same emphasis. John incorporates that emphasis in the stated purpose for writing his book, John 20:31: "These are written that you may believe that Jesus is the Christ, the *Son of God*, and that by believing you may have life in his name."

Many commentators express difficulty identifying the meaning of this messianic title with one of the expressions in this verse. In Isaiah 4:2 Messiah is said to be "the fruit of the land," which they reason has no connection to Messiah. But this objection cannot carry all the weight it is expected to bear. For example, the word "fruit" may be understood to mean a new vitality that God will give to the land of Judah in messianic times, or it could better be taken figuratively to refer to Messiah's origins as being from a human source as well as divine. He was in Mary's womb for nine months, yet he also proved he was from God by showing his ability to forgive sins.

The times spoken of in Isaiah 4:3–4 are those in which Israel will be restored to her land once again. But more than that, she will be washed clean and purged of her sins (4:4). He who is of purer eyes than ours cannot look on sin; therefore it was necessary for him to remove all sin with its stains from his people, before Israel can be remarried to the Lord.

The language of verses 4–5 reflects Israel's experience in the wilderness, where the pillar of cloud and pillar of fire guided and protected them day and night (Exod. 13:20–21). The "cloud of smoke by day and a glow of flaming fire by night" (5b) surely signals the presence and the glory of God once again in the midst of Israel. In fact, verse 5c promises "over all [or 'beyond all'] the glory will be a canopy." The word used for "canopy" is the Hebrew word *huppah*, which is "marriage canopy," under which every Jewish wedding is solemnized, even to this day. Therefore, God is here represented as remarrying Israel. Despite the jarring words in Isaiah 2:6–4:1 that might seem at first glance to imply that God might abandon his ancient covenant with Israel forever, the text instead boldly announces a remarriage will take place.

That is why the "glory [of the Lord]" will be a "shelter and a shade from the heat of the day" (4:6), reminiscent of the cloud of smoke by day and a flaming fire at night. The "Branch of the Lord" will be "beautiful and glorious" in that day to be sure (2).

Conclusions

1. Despite all of Israel and Judah's failures, nevertheless, God will once again take them into a marriage covenant with himself.
2. The nations of the world will annually come in the millennial kingdom to be taught by the Lord and to worship him in Zion, the city of Jerusalem.
3. The Lord will be the supreme judge over the nations and settle all disputes in that day.
4. No longer will military hardware be needed; all weapons will be turned into agricultural implements.
5. Neither will it be necessary to train for war anymore, for peace will be the order of the day.
6. Messiah, the Branch of the Lord, will wash clean believing mortals and purge them of all their sins.

7

The Extent of Messiah's Rule and Reign

Psalm 72:1–17

"[Messiah] will rule from sea to sea . . . to the ends of the earth."

Psalm 72:8

The greatest block of predictive matter concerning the Savior to be found anywhere in the Old Testament," according to J. Barton Payne, is in the book of Psalms.[1] He finds 101 verses of direct messianic prophecies in thirteen different psalms. Other writers tend to be more conservative in their estimates, such as the Lutheran commentator H. C. Leupold, who limits the number of messianic psalms to four: Psalms 22, 45, 72, 110.[2] At the other extreme was St. Augustine, who unfairly treated every psalm as if it were messianic. But his approach violated the basic rules of modern exegesis, for many now believe it is better to rely on the straightforward claims of the text itself.

In my treatment of Messiah in the Psalms,[3] I argue for thirteen messianic psalms: 2, 16, 22, 40, 45, 68, 69, 72, 89, 109, 110, 118, and 132. This is very similar to the list given by James E. Smith,[4] but he argues for sixteen such psalms. Thus he adds Psalms 8, 78:1–2, and 102.

If I were to describe these psalms in the order of their chronological fulfillment in the life of Messiah, I would place them in this order:

David's Greater Son, Messiah—Psalms 89; 132
The Rejection of Messiah—Psalm 118
The Betrayal of Messiah—Psalms 69; 109
The Death and Resurrection of Messiah—Psalms 16; 22
The Written Plan and Marriage of Messiah—Psalms 40; 45
The Triumph of Messiah—Psalms 2; 68; 72; 110

Psalm 72 is called a direct messianic psalm because it uses the future tense throughout the psalm and also because it uses frequent hyperbole. King Solomon, who wrote this psalm according to the ancient heading, could not have fulfilled its terms, even in all his glory. Instead, Solomon's reign can supply only the imagery, language, and line of descent for the one and only proper occupant of the throne in his peaceful and prosperous rule and reign to come.

Psalm 72 is one of the "royal" or "kingship psalms," which Hermann Gunkel (1862–1932) describes in his *Die Psalmen* (1926–28).[5] Gunkel proposes ten royal psalms according to their literary forms: Psalms 2, 20, 21, 28, 45, 72, 101, 110, 132, and 144:1–11, but it does not seem that Psalms 101 or 110 meet his own criteria. Much later, John H. Eaton uses Gunkel's criteria for two of his royal psalms, namely, that they have a Davidic superscription, to develop some twenty-four additional characteristics for this category of psalms, resulting in a list of fifty-four royal psalms which he adds to Gunkel's original ten royal psalms.

Surprisingly, however, nowhere in the New Testament is Psalm 72 quoted or treated as a messianic psalm. For some that would severely limit its messianic usage—that is, those who argue solely from a Christotelic or apostolic approach, meaning that these interpreters require permission to "reinterpret" the text from a New Testament standpoint. Nevertheless, so clear is the picture of the king described in this psalm and so extensive and far-reaching are the boundaries of his rule and reign, not to mention the similarities between this psalm and Isaiah 11:1–5 or Isaiah 60–62, that one cannot deny that Psalm 72 is also messianic and indeed a royal psalm.

Another clue to its messianic interpretation is the use of metaphoric and hyperbolic language that clearly extends the limits of the royal reign well beyond the boundaries of Israel and the times of Solomon, or any other Davidic king for that matter. It is this use of hyperbolic language that appealed to the "Antiochene school," which was founded by Lucian of Antioch (d. AD 312) and who was followed by such imposing names as Theodore of Mopsuestia (ca. AD 350–428), Jerome (ca. AD 347–420), and John Chrysostom (ca. AD 347–407).

The Antiochene school established the model of "*theoria*," which meant in Greek "sight," "insight," "vision," or the lining up of what had happened in the *past* with an analogous final event in the *distant future* so that they could be said to be *one* in meaning, even though they were two or more events in their fulfillments. The work of Bradley Nassif's Fordham University dissertation[6] on the method of *theoria* has been especially helpful in analyzing this psalm.

The Antiochenes stood over against the Alexandrian school, which used the allegorical method of interpreting the Scriptures. But the Antiochian school grounded all meaning in the historical reality of the past, which often served as a mirror by which one could see the future lined up in the same single meaning, so that the past and the distant future were part and parcel of the same single vision.

Julian of Eclanum seems to have best learned to use the principle of *theoria* from Theodore while living with him from AD 421–428, after being exiled from Italy. Theodore demonstrates the method of *theoria* in the way the apostle Paul uses Hosea 1:10 in Romans 9:26 ("And it will come about that, in the place where it is said to them, 'You are my people,' it will be said to them, 'You are sons of the living God'"; my translation). Julian teaches, therefore:

> The apostle wants to show us which rule we must follow in the interpretation of the prophetic books. It is this: That when [we hear the prophets] speaking about the Jews, [and] something is promised that goes behind the small circle of people, yet we see it partly fulfilled in that nation, we know from *theoria* (*per theoriam*) that the promise is given for all people. . . . It will not be appropriate to say that the recall from the Babylonian captivity is predicted according to history, and the liberty given by Christ [is] according to allegory. No. The prophet predicted both things together at one time, jointly (*cum sermo propheticus solide utrumque promiserit*) in order that the mediocrity of the first fulfillment would predict the abundance of the second. . . . So what Hosea was saying about the Babylonian times, Paul [likewise] attributes to the facts of the Savior.[7]

This approach to interpreting the Old Testament prophets is very similar to the method, used by Willis J. Beecher, of "generic interpretation." Beecher does not use the term *theoria*, but he defines his method this way:

> A generic prediction is one which regards an event as occurring in a series of parts, separated by intervals, and expresses itself in language that may apply indifferently to the nearest part, or to the remotest parts, or to the whole—in other words, a prediction which, in applying to the whole of a complex event also applies to . . . its parts.[8]

This is not to say that the Antiochene school or Beecher are teaching "double meaning" or "double sense," as if the historic meaning means one thing and the future fulfillment means another; instead, that is what both are clearly trying to avoid. Therefore, they argue for one sense, one meaning, even though there often are multiple fulfillments of that same single meaning of the text that is shared "hyperbolically" or "analogically."

The Canonical Placement of Psalm 72

Several commentators have investigated why certain psalms are placed on the "seams" or divisions of the five books of the Psalter. They ask, what patterns of organization can be discerned from the placement of the psalms, if there is one to be found at all?

Walter Brueggemann and Patrick Miller[9] note that the placement of Psalm 73, which appears at the beginning of Book III (Pss. 73–89), stands in juxtaposition to Psalm 72, a psalm "by/for Solomon" that ends Book II in the Psalter. If this was done intentionally, why are the two psalms placed back to back? If Psalm 73 is a sapiential or wisdom psalm, as most contend, and Psalm 72 is a royal psalm, does the juxtaposition of the two psalms have more meaning and significance than immediately meets the eye?

G. H. Wilson argues for precisely this point when he claims that there is a progression in the royal psalms placed at the seams of Books I–II of the Psalter.[10] In these psalms it is possible to chart the rise and fall of the Davidic monarchy. Thus, for Wilson, Psalm 2 marks the inauguration of the Davidic covenant, while Psalm 72 marks its transition to future Israelite kings, leaving Psalm 89 (at the end of Book III) to lament the rejection (even if only temporary from an evangelical point of view) of the Davidic kingship. Some think this also explains why the royal psalms play such a small role in Books IV to V when compared to their larger role in Books I–III.

Christopher Seitz has taken this argument one step further.[11] He proposes to view the Davidic house and kingship of God as portrayed in Psalms and Isaiah as being parallel to one another. Therefore, as the Davidic throne *recedes* into the background and then finally *disappears*, as it appears to do from the fall of Jerusalem in 586 BC onward, the kingship of God *rises* in prominence. Accordingly, Psalm 72 is to be viewed as a fading marker of the Davidic line, thereby allowing the emergence of the enthronement psalms about God in Book IV (Pss. 90–106) to take center stage.

It is directly in answer to this pitting the Davidic dynasty against the coming enthronement of Messiah that makes a return to the Antiochian hermeneutic of *theoria* to be so useful. Instead of "reinterpreting" or contrasting the promised throne of David with the rule of Messiah, one can still insist on retaining the full historical setting and meaning of Psalm 72 with its center on the Davidic kingship, while also noting the psalm's hyperbolic enlargement of that concept from the seminal idea as given to David and his house into its final realization in the ultimate Davidic king, the Messiah. The text itself will be the best place to test this thesis.

The Extent of Messiah's Rule and Reign

Text: Psalm 72:1–17

Title: "The Extent of Messiah's Rule and Reign"

Focal Point: Verses 7–8, "In his days the righteous will flourish; prosperity will abound till the moon is no more. He will rule from sea to sea and from the River [Euphrates] to the ends of the earth."

Homiletical Keyword: Characteristics

Interrogative: How? (How should we characterize our enjoyment of the blessings of the extent of the kingdom promised to the Davidic-messianic rule and reign?)

Teaching Aim: To show that Solomon was only one of many in the Davidic line, which would be finally fulfilled in the worldwide rule of Messiah.

Outline

1. Observing How Righteous and Fair the Messiah Is to All—72:1–7
2. Noting How Extensive and Beneficial the Messiah Is to the Whole World—72:8–14
3. Sensing How Prosperous and Blessed Messiah Is to All—72:15–17

Exegetical Study

1. *Observing How Righteous and Fair the Messiah Is to All—72:1–7*

Many have viewed Psalm 72 as composed of four poetic strophes based on what they perceive as the following four characteristics of the king's and Messiah's reign:

1. righteous (72:1–7)
2. universal (72:8–11)
3. beneficial (72:12–14)
4. perpetual (72:15–17)

For example, James Smith argues for these four qualities of Messiah's future reign.[12] But a better case is made by Charles A. Briggs for only three strophes, each beginning with a prayer in verses 1, 8, and 15.[13] In Briggs's view, the three prayers corresponded to Solomon's prayer for wisdom offered at Gibeon and his prayer at the dedication of the temple. This seems to be the best division of the psalm; therefore the suggested exposition of this passage will follow that structure.

The imagery and content of this psalm are prompted by the peaceful and prosperous reign of the grandest monarch Judah ever had, King Solomon. It is this historical reality that had served as the basis for anticipating a surpassing expression of a greater reign in the future—one that had only been seen in modest glimpses by the Davidic King Solomon. It is not as if Solomon cherished the wish that he in his person would finally epitomize or even perhaps be that coming messianic person himself; rather, Solomon speaks here as a prophet who anticipated one who would come after him and who would be greater than he ever was or ever could hope to be (cf. Matt. 12:42).

Psalm 72 begins with a prayer to God that is signaled by its vocative form. "O Elohim!" Elohim is the divine name that in its address embraces all nations and all of creation, along with all its creatures, whereas the name Yahweh usually assumes a personal relationship from the people who are believers. Even though this psalm may originally have been created for a coronation ceremony for Solomon, as some argue, nonetheless much of the content of the verses that follow extend well beyond that setting, so that they can hardly be understood of any earthly monarch except by way of pure "hyperbole."[14] This, of course, is one of the reasons why Christians have treated this psalm as messianic as well as historically referring to Solomon.

With this prayer, Solomon continues with a demand ("give," i.e., "endow," in the imperative mood) that Elohim endow the king with justice. The verbs used here are best understood as future tenses, rather than the jussive forms for "may" or "let." These verbs request that God will indeed grant such a request to "a king" (Hebrew *lemelek*), not "the king." The scope of this request is enlarged by making "a king" parallel to "a son of the king" (Hebrew *leben melek*). The concern of the psalmist is the whole royal house of David as climaxed in Messiah himself.

The only use made of the divine name in this whole psalm is Elohim. Elohim is requested to endow the king with two divinely originated virtues: "God's justices" (note the rare plural) and God's "righteousness." The plural of "justice" probably signifies justice in the fullest form of God's decisions and judgments, while his righteousness points to what is right, harmonious, and normal in all relations between God and mortals as determined by the character and attributes of God. This righteousness is mentioned three times in just three verses (1–3). It includes the concept of God's law and the state of being in conformity with all that is good, excellent, and that which maintains what is "in the right" with the will and work of God. The hope expressed here is that this endowed king will continue to dispense these gifts for a long time to come.

It is at this point that the hyperboles begin to manifest themselves as extending over a duration of a time of peace, prosperity, and divine vindication "as long as the sun" and "as long as the moon" last (5). It is important to recall, however, that this very same concept of perpetuity is what had been promised specifically in the earlier Davidic covenant (2 Sam. 7:13, 16).[15] The psalmist's prayer request, then, is that God will make happen all he had promised to David in the Davidic covenant.

In addition to these requests, the peace and prosperity of the kingly reign are likened to "rain falling on a mown field" (6). This too is not an unexpected metaphor in a Davidic or messianic context, for it had already been used of the refreshing effects of the reign of a Davidic king in 2 Samuel 23:3–4 ("When one rules over men in righteousness, when he rules in the fear of God, he is like . . . the brightness after rain that brings the grass from the earth"). It is worthy of note that the fertility of any country or land is connected to the righteous rule of a just king. It is also important to note how frequently the concepts of "rain," "growth," and "fertility" are linked with the concepts of "right," "righteousness," and "justice" in the Scriptures. These sets of attributes cannot be separated if peace, justice, and righteousness are to prevail in any country.

2. Noting How Extensive and Beneficial Messiah Is to the Whole World—72:8–14

The extent of the just king's kingdom stretches from "sea to sea" and "from the River [Euphrates] to the ends of the earth" (8). This covers everything from the Mediterranean Sea on the west of Israel to the uttermost sea on the earth and from the Euphrates River (for so the Hebrew spelling here demands the Euphrates River) unto the ends of the earth—an obvious set of hyperboles! In part, there is also an allusion to the boundaries of the promised land (Exod. 23:31, where it was announced, "I will establish your borders from the Red Sea [*yam suf*] to the Sea of the Philistines [Mediterranean Sea], and from the desert to the River [Euphrates]"). However, the kingdom of Messiah will far exceed anything ever seen in the Judean line of kings. Messiah's kingdom will reach the fringes of the civilized world, embracing the desert tribes, and it will even subjugate all "enemies," who would suffer defeat as they "lick[ed or bit] the dust" (9). This same defeat had been predicted against Satan himself in the earliest announcement of the promise-plan of God in Genesis 3:14–15, later called the "protoevangelium," and repeated for all the Davidic kings' enemies in Isaiah 49:23 and Micah 7:17 ("[Nations] . . . will lick dust like a snake, like creatures that crawl on the ground").

But there is more: the reign of this righteous king will extend, as we have seen thus far,

1. *geographically* from sea to sea, which is to say around the world;
2. *militarily* over all enemies opposing his reign; but now also add to this that this reign will extend

3. *economically*, as tribute and gifts will be brought from all over the world (v. 10); and

4. *politically*, as all potentates will come under this righteous king's rule and serve him (v. 11).

Nations far and near will come bringing gifts to him, much as the Magi did when Messiah appeared in his first advent. Another example of the nations coming from abroad is "Tarshish" (10), long identified with Tartessos in southern Spain, but more recently as Tarshish in Sardinia. "Sheba" and "Seba" (10) are located respectively in modern Yemen in South Arabia and in an African nation (cf. Gen. 10:7; Isa. 43:3; 45:14).

The blessed king will invest himself on behalf of the "needy," the "afflicted," and the "weak," along with those who are victims of "oppression" and "violence"; in other words, he will take up the cause of those who are destitute and cast aside by society at large (12–14). Their lives ("blood" in v. 14) are precious in that coming king's sight. While King Solomon may have carried out some of this while he was king, it is clear, at least by the end of his reign, the ten northern tribes felt that Solomon had treated them badly, for they felt overtaxed and handled unfavorably in comparison with the tribe of Judah. It is no surprise then that Solomon's son, King Rehoboam, was unsuccessful in addressing the grievances against the later years of Solomon's reign. Moreover, Solomon's reign never took in all the world's needy, poor, and oppressed; someone greater than Solomon was needed to finish the job.

3. Sensing How Prosperous and Blessed Messiah Is to All—72:15–17

For a third time, the psalmist's prayer is enjoined for

1. the unending perpetuation of the Davidic dynasty,
2. the security and economic thriving of the kingship, and
3. the extension of the king's great wealth in all areas of life.

Once the conditions mentioned in verses 12–14 had been met, the longevity of the just and righteous king could be described. This can be illustrated in the gifts that come from the subject nations, such as "gold from Sheba" (15; cf. 1 Kings 10:14–15). Sheba, of course, is the

land from which the queen came to visit and test Solomon's wisdom
(1 Kings 10:1–13). It is located at the southwestern tip of the Arabian
Peninsula in modern Yemen.

Even though God had given fruitfulness to the land of Israel during
Solomon's day, still the prayer about the coming of Messiah was for
days that would be accompanied by an abundance of grain throughout
the land in such proliferation that the stalks of grain would wave just
as plentifully and beautifully as the trees of Lebanon—even from the
most unexpected and desolate places, such as the tops of the mountains (16). As A. A. Anderson puts it,

> This verse (v. 16) and the Psalm as a whole, shows that what we call
> the "moral realm" and the "realm of nature" form one indivisible
> whole to the Israelites. A community which lives according to righ-
> teousness enjoys not only the internal harmony but also prosperity in
> field and flock.[16]

Some read, instead of "his name" in verse 17, "his progeny." But
this is not well supported by the text. The truth of an extensive "seed"
is taught abundantly in other contexts (Isa. 9:2; 49:20; Zech. 2:8 [4]),
but in this context it is the name of the Lord that is lifted high.

The use of the Hebrew Hithpael of the verb *barak*, "to bless" (17b),
is usually rendered reflexively, i.e., "bless themselves," as if all the
nations of the world will see what is happening to Israel as they too
will bless themselves! But this Hebrew form can be read just as well
as a passive form of the verb, "will be blessed," as can be seen in two
of the five instances where it appears in the same promise made in
the Abrahamic covenant (to Abraham: Gen. 12:2–3; 18:18; 22:17–18;
to Isaac: Gen. 26:3–4; and to Jacob: Gen. 28:13–14). To this day,
most commentators remain skeptical about the passive meaning of
the Hebrew Niphal (used in three of the five cases in the patriarchs),
much more so the Hebrew Hithpael (used in two of the five cases).
However, O. T. Allis presents strong evidence to the contrary in his
1927 article, which has not been answered to this day.[17]

This psalm ends Book II of the Psalms with a doxology, in verses
18–20. It attributes to the Lord all the blessings that already have,
or will, come from the reign of God's anointed one. The Lord is the
worker of "marvelous deeds" or "wonders," a word that is also used
of God's works in the plagues of Egypt against Pharaoh.

There is little wonder that Isaac Watts (1674–1748) and James Montgomery (1771–1854) each composed a hymn based on Psalm 72. Watts wrote "Jesus Shall Reign":[18]

> Jesus shall reign where'er the sun
> Does his successive journeys run;
> His kingdom stretch from shore to shore,
> Till moons shall wax and wane no more.

> . . . .

> People and realms of every tongue
> Dwell on his love with sweetest song;
> And infant voices shall proclaim
> Their early blessings on his name.

Montgomery wrote "Hail to the Lord's Anointed":[19]

> Hail to the Lord's Anointed!
> Great David's greater Son;
> Hail in the time appointed,
> His reign on earth begun!
> He comes to break oppression,
> To set the captive free;
> To take away transgression,
> And rule in equity.

Conclusions

1. The words of the psalmist are at once both history and prophecy, for what they see in a vision (*theoria*) holds the historical point of view in unity with the hyperbolic expressions of its ultimate fulfillment.
2. David's line will finally produce a king who will rule with justice and righteousness as he defends the afflicted ones, the poor, and the needy in the last days.
3. Under Messiah's reign, peace, prosperity, and righteousness will be the order in that day.
4. All the kings of the earth will come to bow down before Messiah and offer him their gifts as his rule endures forever.

Part 4

The Day of the Lord and the Beginning of the Nations' Struggle with Israel

The Old Testament prophets often referred to the sovereign plan of God, one which truly included all the nations of the world. Israel was not God's pet, nor did he exercise a chauvinistic attitude toward that nation to the disadvantage of all the other nations. Israel merely was to be the means by which God would bring blessing on all the nations of the earth (Gen. 12:3). The apostle Paul regards the promise about the seed of Abraham, being the means by which God will bless all the nations of the earth, as the substance of the gospel itself (Gal. 3:8).

In the overall plan of God, however, matters will come to a head at a time known as "the day of the Lord," or simply as "that day," or "in the latter days." This "day" is never conceived of as a twenty-four-hour period, but a period of time associated with the second advent of our Lord as he brings the first phase of history to a conclusion, prior to his thousand-year rule on the earth.

It is all marked off by a period, revealed to Daniel, as a time of "seventy weeks." These weeks, which are treated as some 490 "years," are divided into three periods: seven, sixty-two, and one final "week"/ period of seven years of intense tribulation for the nation Israel.

It appears that before the final seven years begin, a Russian-Iranian confederation along with most Arab states will decide to act against Israel in the Gog-Magog plot, but with disastrous results for those nations. God will intervene in a spectacular way, and Israel will be rescued.

In the middle of those final seven years, the antichrist of the western confederation, now leading seven western nations, will break a treaty he has made with Israel, thereby initiating what is known from Scripture as the battle of Armageddon, wherein all the nations of the world will decide to finish what Gog-Magog started against Israel. But this too will end with enormous losses on both sides until the Lord himself arrives in all of his splendor.

The relevant passages need to be treated as whole texts with a full exposition of each chapter for the current people of God, rather than as scattered bits of information garnered from verses found all over the entire Bible. This will give the people of God a foundation from which to approach these matters.

May God's teachers and undershepherds enjoy the power of God's Word as God's men and women are startled by the amount of detail contained in the Old Testament about these coming events.

8

The Arrival of the Day of the Lord

Joel 2:28-3:21

"The day of the Lord is near."

Joel 3:14

The theme of "the day of the Lord" is frequently found in the Old Testament prophets. It might seem as though that day has been delayed too long, not only in the days of the prophets but also in our own day, to be of any real relevance to even those who awaited its arrival in the first Christian century. But in 2 Peter 3:8–10 we are warned,

> But do not forget this one thing, dear friends: With the Lord a day is like a thousand years, and a thousand years are like a day. The Lord is not slow in keeping his promise as some understand slowness. He is patient with you, not wanting anyone to perish, but everyone to come to repentance.
>
> But the day of the Lord will come like a thief. The heavens will disappear like a roar; the elements will be destroyed by fire, and the earth, and everything in it, will be laid bare.

So, we can be sure that that day will indeed come; but *when* will it come? Joel is the one who had the answer. The prophet Joel also knew *upon whom* that day would come, *where* it would occur, and *why* it would fall on those to whom it was directed!

The best place to begin to understand the theme of "the day of the Lord" is in Joel 2:28–3:21. Joel was probably written in the 800s BC (ninth century BC), with almost one-third of his book quoted by other prophets who followed him, for Joel seems to have set up the parameters for this doctrine more than his fellow prophets.[1]

The Arrival of the Day of the Lord

Text: Joel 2:28–3:21

Title: "The Arrival of the Day of the Lord"

Focal Point: Verse 14, "Multitudes, multitudes in the valley of decision! For the day of the LORD is near in the valley of decision."

Homiletical Keyword: Decisions

Interrogative: What? (What are the decisions our Lord has made with regard to the coming day of the Lord?)

Teaching Aim: To teach what the day of the Lord is along with teaching the when, where, and why that day must happen.

Outline

1. God's Outpouring of the Holy Spirit on That Day—2:28–32
2. God's Time for the Day of the Lord—3:1–2d
3. God's Reasons for Bringing the Day of the Lord—3:2e–8
4. God's Opposition to the Nations on That Day—3:9–17
5. God's Blessing as the Day of the Lord Climaxes—3:18–21

Exegetical Study

1. God's Outpouring of the Holy Spirit on That Day—2:28–32

The people of Joel's day had been hit by four major waves or types of locust plagues. These infestations had come as a wake-up call to the people of the land of Israel to repent of their sin and to return to God. Since the people had become insensitive to the preaching of the word of the Lord from his prophets, God was willing to show that he still loved them as he sent this new set of warnings through the events of nature to see if he could arouse them to repentance and spiritual action.

Twice the prophet Joel issues a call to the people to repent, in Joel 1:13–14 and Joel 2:13–14. In the face of all that they were experiencing in the locust infestations and the drought, it was clear that it was high time to repent and to confess their sins to the Lord, for God was obviously giving them a wake-up call to repent.

In Joel 2:18, the people must have repented of their sin, for in that verse, whose four Hebrew verbs ought to be translated in the past tense (and not in the future tense as in the NIV, for example), the Lord "was jealous for his land," "he [then] took pity," he "answered," and he "said" that he would reverse the incursions of the locusts and the savage effects of one wave of these critters after another. The Lord would do this by immediately bringing about a change in nature so that the pastures, now eaten down to the dirt by these locusts, would once again green up (19–27) with newly sprouted grass. In fact, God would send the early and the latter rain, "as before" (23), but "afterward" (28a), he would also "pour out [his] Spirit on all" (28b). *At first*, God would send the needed rains, but *afterward* he would send a downpour of his Holy Spirit.

If the immediate greening of the pastures represented the immediate effect of their repentance and the "now" aspect of the future day of the Lord, there was also a "not yet" aspect that would not be realized until it came to pass "in the last days" (Acts 2:17). The apostle Peter, for instance, is interpreting what Joel meant by his word "afterward" (Joel 2:28) on the day of Pentecost. Even though we tend to think of "the last days" as indicating the time only connected directly with the second coming of Jesus the Messiah, nevertheless, the New Testament teaches us that the "last days" embraces the entire period that extends from the advent of our Lord's first coming all the way up to, and including, the second advent when he will come again. Thus, the book of Hebrews opens its message with the fact that God had spoken "in the past" times by his prophets, but now he has also spoken to us by his son, Jesus, "in these last days" (Heb. 1:1–2). In this way we can see what is meant by "inaugurated eschatology," where there is both a "now" fulfillment in the present time and a "not yet" fulfillment that awaits a distant future.

Accordingly, the outpouring (or "down-pouring") of the Holy Spirit begun at Pentecost (Acts 2) was an *initial* fulfillment of those "last days" or "the day of the Lord." But that was not the end of it by a long shot, for there is a continuing fulfillment all during these days of the church age that extends beyond our day into the future. Thus the church age, too, cannot be the conclusion to those days, for the *ultimate* fulfillment awaits the second coming of Christ when the

Holy Spirit will come as a veritable downpour on the nation of Israel. At that time, the outpouring of the Spirit will also be accompanied by a real cosmic shakeup "in the heaven above and . . . on the earth below" (Acts 2:19–20, quoting Joel 2:30–31).

The term *Pentecost* does not appear in the Old Testament, but it is a term adopted from the Greek language meaning "fifty," where it appears in Acts 2:1; 20:16; and 1 Corinthians 16:8. In the Old Testament, this feast was known as the "Feast of Weeks" (Exod. 34:22; Deut. 16:10; 2 Chron. 8:13) or the "Feast of Harvest" (Exod. 23:16), which came fifty days after the events of Passover.

Later Jewish writers gave even more prominence to this feast than the Old Testament did, for they celebrated it as a time of the giving of the law of God at Sinai. But once Jesus arrived, it became not only an important feast commemorating the giving of the law, but it now celebrated the coming of the Holy Spirit and the giving of the inward law.

Now at Pentecost, the Holy Spirit is poured out in such an avalanche that the contrast between before and after would be like experiencing a normal rainfall versus being under a monsoon or a tropical downpour of the Spirit. This is exactly what the prophets had envisaged in their writings as well. For example, Isaiah 32:14–15 declares,

> The fortress will be abandoned,
>   the noisy cities deserted;
> citadel and watchtower will become a wasteland forever,
>   the delight of donkeys, a pasture for flocks,
> *till the Spirit is poured upon us from on high.* [emphasis mine]

The same concept appears in Isaiah 44:3:

> For I will pour water on the thirsty land,
>   and streams on the dry ground;
> *I will pour out my Spirit on your offspring,*
>   and my blessing on your descendants. [emphasis mine]

The prophet Ezekiel predicts a similar promise in Ezekiel 11:16–19:

> Therefore say: "This is what the Sovereign LORD says: Although I sent them far away among the nations and scattered them among the countries, yet for a little while I have been a sanctuary for them in the countries where they have gone."

> Therefore, say: "This is what the Sovereign LORD says: I will gather you from the nations and bring you back from the countries where you have been scattered, and I will give you back the land of Israel again."
>
> "I will give them an undivided heart and *put a new Spirit in them*; I will remove from them their heart of stone and give them [instead] a heart of flesh." [emphasis mine]

Ezekiel repeats this same promise in Ezekiel 36:27–28; 37:12–14; and 39:28–29. What is most significant is that each of these predictions about the outpouring of the Holy Spirit upon Israel takes place when Israel is back in the land again. And when this happens, the coming of the Spirit will also have healing effects on the land of Israel as well.

However, Joel had predicted that this outpouring of the Spirit would also come on "all flesh" (2:28, translation mine). Surely this includes "sons and daughters," "old men and young men," "men servants" and "maidservants." Joel may have meant to emphasize the fact that these were all Jewish recipients of the outpouring of the Holy Spirit, yet the New Testament universalizes this promise in Acts 2:39 by saying that "the promise is for you and your children and for all who are far off." The expression "all who are far off" is a circumlocution for pointing to the gentiles, as we see in Ephesians 2:13, 17. Moreover, Acts 10:45 settles the matter by declaring that the gentiles are part of the promise: "The circumcised believers who had come with Peter were astonished that the gift of the Holy Spirit had been poured out even on the Gentiles." That agrees well with what Moses had said when his understudy, Joshua, came to him with the report that Eldad and Medad had evidenced the work of the Holy Spirit long after the others in the group of seventy elders had stopped showing any such evidence of the Spirit's work by way of prophesying. Moses replied to his young lieutenant, "Are you jealous for my sake? I wish that all the LORD's people were prophets and that the LORD would put his Spirit on [all of] them!" (Num. 11:29). Moreover, usually the male and female servants in a Jewish home were gentiles in background, so Joel's promise includes "men servants" and "maidservants," a direct promise made also to gentiles.

The results of the outpouring of the Spirit would be realized, among other things, in dreams and visions. All this would take place when the Spirit poured himself out "in those days" (Joel 2:29).

In those same times of the last days, "The sun will be turned to darkness and the moon to blood" (2:30). This will all take place "before the coming of the great and dreadful day of the LORD" (2:31). All who call on the name of the Lord will be saved. But God promises that on Mount Zion and in Jerusalem there will be deliverance (2:32). What a catastrophic day that will be for all who are not believers!

2. God's Time for the Day of the Lord—3:1–2d

We are assured that the day of the Lord will come, but when will it arrive? We are not given a specific date, of course, but we are told where it comes in the course of human history. The dateline Joel places it in is "when I restore the fortunes of Judah and Jerusalem" (3:1). This meant that two dates in history and eschatology are interrelated: the day of Israel's return to her land and the day of the Lord's second advent. This return to the land must be more than a return from the Babylonian exile. To be sure, on May 15, 1948, the Jewish state was created by the United Nations partition of Palestine. But even in that unique event, the old city of Jerusalem still remained in the hands of the Jordanians, so it did not fulfill the time of the "restor[ation of] the fortunes of Judah and Jerusalem" (3:1). But that too changed (for the most part) in the Six-Day War of 1967, when Israel gained control over much of the land of Israel including the old city of Jerusalem.

But the tenuousness of the Jewish state was later demonstrated during the Yom Kippur War in October 1973. Egypt and Syria chose to attack Israel during her most holy day, the Day of Atonement. At first the Arabs made strong advances, but Israel soon saw the battle reverse its direction as she began to penetrate northeast toward Damascus as well as southwest into Egypt. As the cease-fire was declared, Israel returned some of the captured territory to the Arabs.

However, if we wish to know where we are in the prophetic calendar, we need to keep our eyes on Israel, for they are God's timepiece. But it is now clear historically that the return from the Babylonian captivity did not introduce the day of the Lord. Another exile, which began with the fall of the second temple in AD 70, has continued up until the present hour in the Jewish Diaspora.

The nations on whom the day of the Lord will fall are generally those who persecute Israel. God will enter into judgment with them by bringing them down into the "Valley of Jehoshaphat" (3:2), a valley generally meant to indicate a place where the "LORD judges" them. Nation after nation is mentioned as being the object of God's judgment. For example, in Obadiah, the Edomites are singled out as the archenemies and persecutors of Israel (Obad. 15, cf. 8–10). In Isaiah, it is the Babylonians who are listed (Isa. 13:6, 9). In Jeremiah and Ezekiel, it is the Egyptians (Jer. 46:10; Ezek. 30:2–4). In the prophet Daniel, Antiochus IV Epiphanes seems to be the "king who will do as he pleases" as a type of the coming antichrist (Dan. 11:36–38). But in the book of Joel, the Phoenicians and Philistines are the enemies of the covenant people of God (Joel 3:4–8). What a long list of nations this grows to be, with others we have mentioned: Edomites, Egyptians, Assyrians, Babylonians, Persians, Greeks, Romans, Russians, Nazis, and Arabs. Even though these nations have been judged in their own time, a time for a final judgment is reserved for them at the end-time. This will take place during the great tribulation in Daniel's seventieth week, climaxed in the battle of Armageddon. The question, of course, is why this future judgment must take place. There are four reasons God gives as to why this must occur, which are discussed in the next section.

3. God's Reasons for Bringing the Day of the Lord—3:2e–8

The prophet Joel gives four reasons why the nations are to be judged. They are guilty for the things they perpetrated upon Israel, and that is why they are the objects of God's wrath in the day of the Lord:

1. They scattered the Jewish people among the nations (3:2e).
2. They partitioned and divided up the land of Israel (3:2f).
3. They made slaves out of the Jewish people (3:3).
4. They carried off the sacred vessels belonging to the temple of the Lord (3:5).

Israel was scattered, of course, mainly because of her own sins against God. Even the Talmud understood that the persecutions of the Jewish people by Rome came by God's permission as a result of Israel's own sin. Nevertheless, all the other nations will suffer in the day of the Lord because they enforced this scattering of the nation of Israel. And, as if the exile of the northern kingdom of Israel in 721/722 BC and the southern kingdom in 586 BC, or even the exile enforced by Rome after the events of AD 70 and 135, were not enough, Jesus in his prophetic discourse on the Mount of Olives speaks of another time when Israel will flee in the end-days, as all the gentile nations will be summoned to fight Israel by their world leader, the antichrist. Jesus teaches, "So when you see standing in the holy place 'the abomination that causes desolation,' spoken of through the prophet Daniel . . . then let those who are in Judea flee to the mountains" (Matt. 24:15; cf. Dan. 9:27; 11:31; 12:11). However, Israel will quickly be rescued even in this end-time fleeing, for soon the nations will be punished in that day of the Lord, ushered in by his second coming.

The second encroachment of the gentile nations on Israel can be seen in the way they partitioned the land of Israel. In the Assyrian record, Sargon II records, "Samaria I besieged and took . . . 27,290 inhabitants I carried away. . . . I set up again [Samaria] and made [it] more populous than before. People from other lands which I had taken I settled there." That account agrees with the one in 2 Kings 17:23–24:

> The LORD removed them from his presence, as he had warned through all his servants the prophets. So the people of Israel were taken from their homeland into exile in Assyria, and they are still there.
>
> The king of Assyria brought people from Babylon, Cuthah, Avva, Hamath and Sepharvaim and settled them in the towns of Samaria to replace the Israelites. They took over Samaria and lived in its towns.

This is why the Samaritans of Jesus's day were regarded as aliens in the land previously inhabited by the Jewish people. But that was not the last time the people were to be deported and the land divided. The Roman general Titus and the emperor Hadrian divided up the land of Israel after the Jewish revolt of AD 70 and the Bar Kokbah revolt of AD 135. Daniel 11:39 seems to say that the antichrist will do the same thing: "He will attack the mightiest fortresses with the help of a foreign god and will greatly honor those who acknowledge him. He will make them rulers over many people and will distribute the land at a price." But all of this will be overruled by the hand of the Sovereign God, who has already granted the land to Israel. In this case, these nations will have to face God himself.

The third offense that stirs up the anger of God against these nations is the unjust act of making slaves of the Jewish people. So impudent were these nations that Joel 3:3–6 says that a boy was bartered as a payment for a harlot and a girl was given as the price of a bottle of wine. Such slave trade was carried out not only by the Greeks in later times but also by Greece with Tyre in an earlier day. Jewish people were also later sold as slaves in the Maccabean civil war, and Titus sold Jews into slavery after Jerusalem had fallen in

AD 70. In fact, the Coliseum in Rome was built largely by the labor of Jewish slaves who were captured after Jerusalem fell. Later in the Bar Kokbah revolt of AD 135, so many Jewish people were sold into slavery that the slave markets were glutted. The industry of human trafficking is still a modern scandal as people continue to be sold into sexual slavery around the world every day!

The nations, in the fourth place, are to be judged because they robbed the treasuries of Judah, things that were privately owned and things that were part of the sacred trust of the temple. Even if Jerusalem was not yet robbed in the ninth century BC, which is where we have placed this prophecy, the words of Joel are accurate as predictions of what took place in 586 and 165 BC, as well as what took place in AD 70.

4. God's Opposition to the Nations on That Day—3:9–17

In verses 9–12, Joel reverses the great figurative language, used by the prophets Isaiah and Micah (Isa. 2:4; Mic. 4:3). Apparently it is not time as yet for the beating of swords into plowshares and spears into pruning hooks. That will come in the messianic reign of the Lord Jesus after this final battle is concluded. Instead, in this situation it is time for the reverse: plowshares must be beat into swords and pruning hooks must be rendered into spears—in other words, the manufacture of military hardware.

It will be a time for rousing the nations to battle in the Valley of Jehoshaphat where the Lord "will sit to judge all the nations on every side" (12). Joel urges that it is time for the harvest; so let the "sickle" swing, and begin trampling the grapes in the winepress, for the vats are figuratively full of grapes, meaning they are full of the "wickedness" of the people (13), which must now be trampled in judgment.

Both Joel and Jesus see the battle of Armageddon as culminating in the vicinity of Jerusalem, even though it begins in the area much to the north and west near Megiddo in the Plain of Esdraelon. The forces that are aroused against Israel are those that belong to the antichrist, the leader of what many believe to be a reconstitution of the revived Roman Empire. Jesus teaches,

Immediately after the distress of those days
   "the sun will be darkened,
      and the moon will not give its light;
   the stars will fall from the sky,
      and the heavenly bodies will be shaken."

At that time the sign of the Son of Man will appear in the sky, and all the nations of the earth will mourn. They will see the Son of Man coming on the clouds of the sky, with power and great glory. And he will send his angels with a loud trumpet call, and they will gather his elect from the four winds, from one end of heaven to the other. (Matt. 24:29–31)

Joel also predicts that the Lord will "roar from Zion and thunder from Jerusalem" (3:16a–c) as the sky and the earth tremble. However, the Lord himself will "be a refuge for his people, a stronghold for the people of Israel" (3:16d–e). The prophet Zechariah sees and describes the same event in his book (14:1–4), as does the apostle John on the island of Patmos in Revelation 19:11–16. The nations will by now have had their last fling against the land and the people of Israel, for they will be soundly defeated for the last time. Then after this battle, the Lord will set up his throne in freshly delivered Jerusalem. Then will all know that "I, the LORD your God, dwell in Zion, my holy hill. Jerusalem will be holy; never again will foreigners invade her" (Joel 3:17).

5. God's Blessing as the Day of the Lord Climaxes—3:18–21

The day of the Lord in this section is also called "in that day" (18). This is not unusual, for the Hebrew prophets often used the expression "in that day" instead of the full title "the day of the Lord." In fact, this shortened form appeared so frequently, that no other modifiers were needed for the prophet's audience, for the pointing to a particular day meant a time when God would act in judgment and blessing, depending on the state of the receiver.

Just as there were four reasons for divine judgment on the nations in the previous section, so this final section of the prophet Joel describes four blessings God is to pour out on the covenant people (3:18–21). These are the blessings:

1. the healing of the land of Israel (3:18),
2. the punishment of all of Israel's enemies (3:19),
3. the designation of the land to Israel for all times to come (3:20), and
4. the pardon of Israel and the dwelling of God in the land (3:21).

The first blessing promises the healing of the land of Israel so that there will come an ecological balance between the physical creation and the spiritual nature of the hearts of the people. Ever since the fall of Adam and Eve, the created world has been impacted, but Romans 8:20–23 notes that creation presently groans in travail, waiting for the hope of the second coming of our Lord. Even now, whenever revival breaks out with evidence of repentance by God's people, *substantial* healing of nature can accompany it as a pledge of what will happen in that final day.

Joel is not alone in predicting a healing of the land "in that day," for the prophet Amos sees the same thing in Amos 9:11–15. In his way of putting it, the crops will be so full in those days that the one plowing the ground will overtake the one reaping the fields, and the one treading out the grapes will be overlapped by the one sowing seed. Amos promises, by the inspiration of the Holy Spirit, that God will "plant" his people Israel in the land, and "never again" will they "be uprooted from the land [God has] given them" (Amos 9:15). This will be a transformed land to say the least.

The second blessing spells the end of enemy hostilities against Israel (Joel 3:19). Egypt and Edom are both listed here because they are traditional enemies of the people of God. This will end the Arab-Jewish conflict, a feud that goes all the way back to the days of Isaac and Ishmael (Gen. 16:11–12). The Edomites, of whom Joel speaks, are the descendants of Esau (the twin brother of Jacob), as are the Arab peoples in general. In the Jewish Talmud and the Midrash, the rabbis also use the term "Edom/Esau" to refer to Rome, which may go too far since an Arab equivalence seems to be far enough.

The third blessing predicts that in the aftermath of the day of the Lord, Israel would have her land secured for her forevermore (Joel 3:20). It is one of the wonders of history that a nation could be out of existence for over two thousand years, but come back into life again on May 15, 1948. This cannot be attributed to some movement, such as the movement of Zionism; but it must be due to the favor and the action of Almighty God. In case some doubt the stability and durability of this restoration, more than four wars since 1948 have reinforced the fact that "Judah will be inhabited forever" (20). Thus, the War of Independence of 1948 was followed by the Sinai Campaign in 1956, the Six-Day War in 1967, and the Yom Kippur War of 1973. Nevertheless, the State of Israel still exists in spite of the heavy odds against it.

The fourth and final blessing in this section of Joel comes in verse 21. Today, over six million Jewish people live in Israel, out of some fourteen million worldwide. In the day that the bones of Israel will be reassembled (see chapter 4 on Ezek. 37), God will give a new heart and a new spirit for Israel's heart of stone (Ezek. 11:19–20). The Jewish people are already returning in mass to the land of Israel, but what about a spiritual transformation?

The prophet Zechariah predicts a time when all Israel will look on the One they had pierced, and the result will be a deep mourning for what they had missed (Zech. 12:10; Rev. 1:7). Yes, "on that day a fountain will be opened to the house of David and the inhabitants of Jerusalem, to cleanse them from sin and impurity" (Zech. 13:1). With this cleansing and repentance, the golden age of Messiah's reign will arrive. And "the LORD [will dwell] in Zion" (Joel 3:21).

Conclusions

1. The day of the Lord promises an outpouring of the Holy Spirit upon Israel and all who will trust in him.
2. That day is set for the time when God restores the fortunes of Judah and Jerusalem by bringing them back to their land.
3. God is angry with the nations for the way they have treated Israel contrary to his instructions.
4. The day of the Lord will bring judgment on all the nations, but it will be a time when he provides a refuge for all who trust him, in Israel and in the world.
5. God will pour out four blessings on Israel that will secure the fruitfulness of her land once again, the destruction of her enemies, the return of Israel to her land along with God's pardon of her sin, and his promise to dwell in Zion.

9

Gog and Magog

Ezekiel 38–39

"O Gog, I will bring you against my land."

Ezekiel 38:16

Few recent books are as fascinating as Joel C. Rosenberg's *Epicenter*[1] when it comes to viewing what Scripture has to say about the big changes that are coming to the world and the effect they will have in both Israel and the world. His graphic depiction of current events against the backdrop of the prophecies in Scripture makes for some very exciting reading to say the least.

He begins, as I do, with the promise-plan of God and its involvement with the people of Israel. The unnatural hatred against the Jewish people is hard to explain historically unless it is also connected with the fact that God has made Israel the agents through whom he would bless the world with the Messiah (Gen. 12:2–3, 7)—the Savior of the world. The list of names of those who in political authority have recently tried to eradicate the Jewish people grows longer and fiercer with almost each passing day: Adolph Hitler, Vladimir Lenin, Joseph Stalin, Osama bin Laden, and so on.

But things will not end well for the nations that press their attack against Israel, for in the end, what they are doing is nothing less than an attack on God and his plan for time and eternity. In one great push, an axis of nations from that part of the world will make one huge incursion into the land of Israel, but that will call for the response of God himself. The carnage, bloodshed, and loss of life and power will be unrivaled up to that point in history. This will be at once one of the darkest, and yet also one of the brightest, days of all history, as God settles the issue in a startling way. Such is the predicted fortunes of the War of Gog and Magog against Israel in the end of the days of history's ongoing time line.

Gog and Magog's War against Israel

Text: Ezekiel 38:1–39:29

Title: "Gog and Magog's War against Israel"

Focal Point: Ezekiel 38:16, "In days to come, O Gog, I will bring you against my land, so that the nations may know me when I show myself holy through you before their eyes."

Homiletical Keyword: Predictions

Interrogative: What? (What are the predictions of what God is going to do as he puts a huge stop to the otherwise steady stream of attacks on the nation of Israel over the course of history?)

Teaching Aim: To demonstrate that God, for his own name's sake, will sensationally rescue Israel when all other sources of help fail.

Outline

1. Our God Will Soundly Defeat Gog and His Allies—38:1–23
   1.1. The Allies of Gog—38:1–6
   1.2. The Purpose and Motives of Gog's War—38:7–13
   1.3. The Advances of Gog—38:14–16
   1.4. The Judgment on Gog—38:17–23
2. Our God Will Easily Dispose of Gog—39:1–29
   2.1. The Slaughter of Gog—39:1–8
   2.2. The Loot Taken from Gog—39:9–10
   2.3. The Burial of Gog—39:11–16
   2.4. The Display of the Glory of God—39:17–29

Exegetical Study

1. Our God Will Soundly Defeat Gog and His Allies—38:1–23

1.1. THE ALLIES OF GOG—38:1–6[2]

God's word came to his prophet Ezekiel concerning an enigmatic person and country known respectively as "Gog" and "the land of Magog" (1). Generally there is little consensus on the interpretation of the name "Gog," but a host of interpreters have given it their best attempt to unravel the meaning of the one to whom it refers. Gog's homeland, "Magog," is the name either of a people or a geographical location (also in Ezek. 39:6). Elsewhere, the name "Magog" is found only in Genesis 10:2, with its parallel in 1 Chronicles 1:5, where Magog is the second son of Japheth along with Gomer, Madai, Javan, Tubal, Meshech, and Tiras. Both the names of Gog and Magog, however, appear to be a fixed pair of names for two of those who are involved in one of the final eschatological battles of history.

In this text, Gog is depicted as the "prince" who is over "Rosh" (*rosh* is also rendered as "chief prince" in the NIV), Meshech, and Tubal (2). There is no little amount of ink spilled over the identity of "Rosh" as well, for it has often been equated with the name of "Russia," a name from northern Viking derivation for the region of the Ukraine in the Middle Ages. Some have attempted to equate "Rosh" with the names of Rashu/Reshu/Arashi in neo-Assyrian annals. Others attempt to link "Rosh" with "Rus," a Scythian tribe inhabiting the northern Taurus Mountains according to Byzantine and Arabic writings. The Scythians were those who were spread over some of the republics of the former Soviet Union, especially those in central Asia. The identity of "Rosh" must remain open, for the evidence is far from conclusive.

Gog's other confederates are Meshech and Tubal, whose names do appear in the list of those with whom Tyre trades (Ezek. 27:13), and who also are among the slain in Sheol (Ezek. 32:26). "Persia" is the first country identified as a future ally of this northern threat, which today would be the land of Iran, Pakistan, and Afghanistan. They are followed by "Cush," who settled in Africa, possibly in "Ethiopia" (or possibly extending to Sudan or Eritrea). That is how the first-century Jewish historian Josephus identifies them as well. "Put" is also identified by Josephus as Libya, with possible extensions into Algeria and Tunisia. "Gomer" is more difficult to identify, for he too appears in Genesis 10 as a son of Japheth. Josephus reminds us that the Greeks called the Galatians "Gomerites," thus we may be talking about those who hailed from Turkey. Others identify this name as referring to the inhabitants of Gaul in France and Spain. Genesis 10:3 identifies one of Gomer's relatives as Ashkenaz, a term used in our day for the Jews in the lands of Germany, Austria, and Poland. The Talmud, however, says the Gomerians were Germans. So, that is where the matter stands to this day. "Beth-togarmah" has been linked by the Greeks with the Phrygians, part of western Asia Minor, later known as Turkey. There seems also to be many other nations not mentioned, but who are fully allied with Gog (Ezek. 38:6) as well.

All these nations and more form a future anti-Israelite coalition with their leader, Gog, coming from the northern region, perhaps Russia. It is interesting to note that the nation of Iran (which includes present-day Pakistan and Afghanistan as well) gets first mention and that most of Gog's allies are countries that are today predominantly Islamic.

1.2. The Purpose and Motives for Gog's War—38:7–13

It is clear from this list, and from the text of Ezekiel, that Israel will seem to be overwhelmed by the enormous number of nations set against her. So huge is their number that they appear to be more like a "cloud" or a "storm" (9). They are depicted by Ezekiel as "coming from [their] place in the far north" (15). The allusion to the "far north" also points to a Russian-led confederation, for Moscow is almost directly north of Jerusalem on a modern map.

This enormous assemblage of forces is instructed to "get ready; be prepared, you and all the hordes gathered about you" (7). They will all be called to arms "after many years," "in future years" to "invade a land that has recovered from war, whose people were gathered from many nations [back] to the mountains of Israel, which had long been desolate. They had been brought out from the nations, and now all of them live in safety" (8). Surely this description easily fits Israel as the object of their assault.

As this horde of troops assembles for war against Israel, the troops will "devise an evil scheme" (10). They imagine that a "land of unwalled villages" and towns "without gates and bars" will be easy to conquer (11).

These nations anticipate an enormous amount of loot—nations from as far away as "Sheba and Dedan," which scholars usually identify with the persons living in the Arabian peninsula, including Saudi Arabia, Yemen, Oman, Kuwait, and the United Arab Emirates (the southern extremity), and the "merchants of Tarshish," which is identified with the area we now call by the name of southern Spain (the western extremity). But it is of more than passing interest that Canada, Britain, and the United States are not listed as participating in this attack on Israel—nor do they apparently offer any assistance to help Israel either! In fact, no nation is listed as offering to come to the rescue of Israel, for she must fight this battle alone—except for the majestic presence of the living God.

But there can be no doubt about the object of the attack, for the nations attacking Israel will come "to the mountains of Israel" (38:8; 39:2, 4), where they will die. If the mountains referred to here are the mountains on Israel's northern border, then modern-day Syria, Lebanon, and the Golan Heights, north of Jordan, are likewise indicated as participants in this battle. As usual, the area from which these Russian-Iranian forces attack is from the north.

1.3. The Advances of Gog—38:14–16

This Russian-Iranian horde will descend, as we have noted, from the north, "riding on horses" (15). No doubt, we must understand here perhaps the modern equivalent for the use of horses, such as tanks and the like, for they would otherwise have had no meaning to those of Ezekiel's day. There is, however, the possibility that weather conditions and strategic reasons may force the use of horses where mechanized equipment would be impossible!

Even though this alliance of nations will think that it was their idea to invade Israel, the living Lord told the prophet Ezekiel that "I will bring you [Gog] against my land" (16). The reason God will allow Gog to lead such an avalanche of troops against Israel is "so that the nations may know me when I show myself holy through you before their eyes" (16).

Joel Rosenberg speculates that Israel, in her loneliness and estrangement from the family of nations, may consider a preemptive strike called by some "the Samson Option." In that option, if Israel is convinced that she is about to be destroyed, she will choose to pull the house down on herself, as Samson did, and take her enemies with her to the grave. Atomic weapons could all of a sudden go flying toward Moscow, Tehran, Damascus, Tripoli, Khartoum, and such similar cities. Such a strike would invite a similar retaliatory response from some of those who are also part of the enemy nuclear club. Whether there will be any preemptive strikes on Israel's part or not, the point is that this will be a war unlike any we have seen thus far in history.

1.4. THE JUDGMENT ON GOG—38:17–23

God reminds Israel that for centuries past he had sent his servants the prophets to call Israel to repentance and a forsaking of the evil they loved so much, but without much success (17). Therefore, at the time when Gog attacks Israel, the blasting wrath of God will evidence itself in an earthquake of momentous proportions. The epicenter for that earthquake will be in Israel, but its shock waves and effects will be felt around the world (19). As a result of this earthquake, "mountains will be overturned, the cliffs will crumble and every wall will fall to the ground" (20). Does this mean that the earthquake will be so fierce that it will interrupt the flow of gas and oil from the Middle East and central Asia to Europe and to other parts of the world?

So confusing will the situation be that "every man's sword will be against his brother" (21). The enemy, instead of fighting against Israel, will start fighting each other as they did in the day of Gideon's victory. The Russian and Muslim forces will end up firing on each other.

But as if that were not enough, God will add to the discomfort to show his estimate of the motives and purposes of the attacking nations. God will "pour down torrents of rain, hailstones and burning sulfur on [Gog] and his troops and on all the nations with him" (22). Such firestorms from God recall the judgment God rained down on Sodom and Gomorrah in Genesis 19. In this way God will exhibit his "greatness and . . . holiness" as he makes himself known before all these pagan nations: they will surely realize that he is "the LORD" (23).

2. Our God Will Easily Dispose of Gog—39:1–29

2.1. THE SLAUGHTER OF GOG—39:1–8

God states once again that he is against this coalition of attackers on Israel (1). This alliance of nations will massively move toward "the mountains of Israel" (2), but they will also die "on [those same] mountains" (4).

The second verb in verse 2 is an inexplicable hapax legomenon (i.e., a word that appears only once in the Bible). Rather than understanding it as a verb related to an Ethiopic word, or some unusual form of a Hebrew verb, the Authorized Version as well as medieval lexicographers more adequately understood it as derived from the Hebrew *shisha*, "to leave a sixth part." If that reading is the correct reading, then, as Joel Rosenberg has suggested, five-sixths of this coalition will be destroyed, leaving only a sixth part or about 17 percent. If those numbers are sustained as the true reading of the text, then the slaughter of Gog will be horrendous indeed—some 83 percent loss of the Russian-Iranian confederacy!

In the recent past, there have been several modern anti-Israelite alliances, but each lacked precise portions of what is predicted in this Gog-Magog War. For example, there was such a war in 1948, but neither Russia nor Iran participated. Again, in the Six-Day War of June 1967 Israel was attacked, but Russia only provided the military equipment, yet she herself did not participate. Neither did the Yom Kipper War of October 1973 qualify, as, once more, those afar only gave military assistance and help. Though the Russian Soviets seemed to be the major sponsors of the trouble, they did not directly participate.

From this day forward, God will "no longer let [his] holy name be profaned" (7). By this one almighty act of deliverance of Israel and the destruction of the coalition, "the nations will know that [he is] the Holy One in Israel" (7). All can be certain that all of this will surely take place, for "[t]his is the day [God] has spoken of" long ago (8).

2.2. The Loot Taken from Gog—39:9–10

So overwhelming will be the victory and triumph of Israel over this Russian-Iranian coalition that after God steps in and decisively defeats the hostile alliance, those who live in the towns and villages of Israel will "go out and use the weapons for fuel and burn them up" (9a). There will be enough there so that Israel will have fuel for "seven years" (9d). The Israelites will have no need to gather wood from their fields or to cut down forests (10). In a massive turnaround, those who had planned on looting Israel will now themselves be looted by Israel, according to the solid declaration of the Lord.

2.3. The Burial of Gog—39:11–16

The carnage from this battle will be beyond anyone's ability to describe it. For instance, in the valley used to travel eastward to the Dead Sea, a blockage will prevent future travelers because of hordes of bodies and corpses that are buried there (11). This massive burial site will result in the valley being renamed to mean something like "the Hordes of Gog" (11), perhaps a wordplay from "the Valley of Hamon-Gog" to "Ge-Hinnom," which translates as "the Valley of Hinnom." That was the site where Molech worshipers in Israel had previously sacrificed their children to the god Molech (Jer. 2:23).

The topic raised in Ezekiel 39:12 is expanded in verses 14–16. The purification of the land of Israel is accomplished by a standing commission appointed to survey the whole land of Israel to spot any remains of unburied bones or carcasses (14a). These men are to canvass the entire land of Israel (14b) in search of any remains of the vanquished foe. Whenever these inspectors spot a human bone, they will "set up a marker beside it until the gravediggers [will take it and bury] it in the Valley of Hamon Gog" (15). All of these bodies, and the disparate bones separately scattered over the surface of the land, were buried in a city called "Hamonah," meaning "horde" (16).

2.4. THE DISPLAY OF THE GLORY OF GOD—39:17–29

In the meantime, a summons goes out to "every kind of bird and all the wild animals" (17). In a most gruesome sight, which is hard even to conceive, a sacrificial feast of unusual proportions is prepared on the mountains of Israel. For the slain that lay in heaps on the mountains of the land are devoured by carnivorous birds and scavenging wild animals (17–19). Ezekiel 38:22 also mentions a divinely sent plague that will be enacted as the war commences, but how much can be attributed to the plague and how much to the war itself is not singled out in the text.

Twice the Lord identifies himself as the One who had prepared this feast (39:17, 19). This is similar to the day when Yahweh celebrates his vengeance over Edom in Isaiah 34:6–8 and in Zephaniah 1:7. The blood of "heroes" and of "princes" is available for all who come to this slaughter.

Ezekiel 39:21–29 completes this section and renders God's final word on what is to take place in that coming day. Especially in verses 23–24, the Gog-Magog War is treated as something that is now over and in the distant past. It will be clear by then that Israel had gone into exile because of her sin and her unfaithfulness to the Lord. It is for these reasons that her offenses and uncleanness had to be dealt with.

But thanks be to God, Israel will by then have been brought back from her captivity (25) and will have been shown God's enormous compassion for her. As a result of God's act of love, Israel will forget her shame and her unfaithfulness (26a). Now the people can live in their land in safety, a remarkable change from the former years of her existence in the land (26b). Israel will have returned back home from all the countries of her enemies (27). None will have been left behind (28). God will no longer hide his face from them, but instead will pour out his Spirit on the house of Israel (29).

Conclusions

1. The Gog-Magog War against Israel will be one of a northern nations' axis with the Arab-Islamic world to defeat the Jewish people in Israel once and for all, but it will turn out as a poorly planned conquest ending in total defeat for those attacking nations.
2. God himself will dramatically intervene in this battle so that the enemy will be destroyed in numbers never seen in the history of fighting.
3. God will demonstrate his greatness and holiness to such a degree that all the nations will be forced to acknowledge that he alone is the Lord of lords and King of kings.
4. The house of Israel will finally see that there is no one like the Lord their God as they are dramatically delivered by the Lord himself, despite the refusal of any nations to come to Israel's defense.

Part 5

The Events
of the Last Seven Years
and the Arrival
of the Western Confederacy

The only chronological hook, of sorts, for the timing of some of the eschatological events at the close of history was given to us by the prophet Daniel as he was reading the prophet Jeremiah. Jeremiah had been told that the people of Judah would remain in captivity in Babylon for seventy years. Daniel, sensing that the seventy years' time was almost up, asked God about these seventy years and wanted to know whether the people of Judah would now be released to go back to their land once again.

God answered Daniel by telling him that there were another "seventy 'sevens'" (Dan. 9:24) that were determined for Daniel, his people, and their holy city Jerusalem. These seventy "sevens" or seventy "weeks" are generally understood to mean that God had another 490 years in which he would deal with Daniel and his people, but these 490 years apparently were not years that would occur one after another in succession in every case. There would be at least one break in this string of years between the sixty-ninth and seventieth "week" of seven years, in which "the Anointed One will be cut off" and the city and the sanctuary would be destroyed (Dan. 9:26).

Our understanding of these two interrupting events, which came between the sixty-ninth and seventieth weeks of years, in turn pointed to the death of Messiah around AD 30 and the destruction of the temple in AD 70. If that is the correct way to understand these two notices in Daniel, and if it is authorized by the phrase "*after* the sixty-two weeks [period]" (26) to indicate a break that has continued from that day until now, then there will be a seven-year period of unusual divine activity as history moves toward the second coming of Messiah.

First, the western nations will be led by one who is elsewhere called the "antichrist." Secondly, he will make a covenant with Israel, which apparently allows Israel to build the third temple, perhaps sharing the very temple platform where the Dome of the Rock is now located, only perhaps on its northern end as it lined up with the famous Eastern Gate. However, in the middle of those seven years, antichrist will break that covenant with Israel and the battle of Armageddon will begin as all the nations of the world come to put a final end to the annoying question of what to do with the Jewish people. That move, however, will be the final straw for all the gentile nations of earth, as God moves dramatically to demonstrate that he is the Sovereign Lord over all.

These then are the topics addressed in the next four chapters.

10

The Seventy Weeks of Daniel

Daniel 9:24–27

"Seventy sevens are decreed for your people and your holy city."

Daniel 9:24

In spite of its popularity in some circles, Daniel 9:24–27 continues to be one of the most difficult passages in the book to interpret to the satisfaction of all interpreters. Most who attempt to tackle this passage begin by quoting the 1927 observation by James A. Montgomery:

> The history of the exegesis of the 70 Weeks is the Dismal Swamp of O.T. Criticism. . . . [T]he trackless wilderness of assumptions and theories in the efforts to obtain an exact chronology fitting into the history of Salvation, after these 2,000 years of infinitely varied interpretations, would seem to preclude any use of the 70 Weeks for the determination of a definite prophetic chronology.[1]

None of these problems have stopped the flow of scholarly commentary on Daniel 9:24–27, or the search for a "definite prophetic chronology." It is clear, nevertheless, that the passage bristles with one issue after another. Therefore, having been forewarned, we too shall wade into the alleged "Dismal Swamp" and this "trackless wilderness," but we will do so with extreme caution.

The Contents of the Prophecy

There are at least ten major items covered in this text. First, the whole passage relates to Daniel's people, Israel, and the "holy city" of Jerusalem (24). That is stated clearly, but is often forgotten. Second, there is mention made of "the Anointed One" and the "ruler" who shall come to destroy the city and the sanctuary (25). Are these two different individuals or the same person? Third, many interpreters and most versions of the Bible render the words of verses 24–26 in such a way as to make two segments of these seventy "weeks" of "sevens," consisting of a period of sixty-nine weeks and one week to follow, instead of three segments of a seven-week period, a sixty-two-week period, and a one-week period. Fourth, are the seventy "sevens" or "weeks" a reference to days, months, or years? And if they refer to years, as most conclude, are these "solar years" of 365 1/4 days, or are these so-called "prophetic years" of 360 days in each year? Fifth, who is "the Anointed One" who will come at the end of the sixty-two "sevens" (25)? Sixth, who is the coming "ruler" who will establish a covenant with many for one week (27), who, seventh, breaks that covenant in the middle of the week, i.e., in the middle of the seven-year period? Eighth, what is the abomination of desolation (27) that this "ruler" will set up in the wing of the temple? Ninth, what is the end point where that "ruler" ceases to operate as decreed (27)? And tenth, to what do the six purposes of the predicted seventy weeks pertain?

This list by no means exhausts all the questions one can raise in this passage. For example, one could also ask: What are the *termini* set for each of the sets of numerical elements? Are these "weeks" contiguous, or are there gaps between each group of the seven, sixty-two, and the one? Is the Masoretic tradition (though later in time) of accentuation (i.e., punctuation) correct for determining the clausal structure of the passage, or are the earlier Theodotion, Vulgate, and Syriac versions to be preferred when it comes to combining the numerical elements of the seven and sixty-two weeks into one unit? Does the word "after" in verse 26 indicate a gap of time between the first sixty-nine weeks and the coming of the seventieth week? If so, how long can that gap be extended? Does it extend up to and include the present day?

Understanding the Seventy Weeks of Daniel

Text: Daniel 9:24–27

Title: "Understanding the Seventy Weeks of Daniel"

Focal Point: Verse 24, "Seventy 'sevens' are decreed for your people and your holy city to finish transgression, to put an end to sin, to atone for wickedness, to bring in everlasting righteousness, to seal up a vision and prophecy and to anoint the Most Holy Place."

Homiletical Keyword: Predictions

Interrogative: How? (How will we understand the predictions of Daniel's seventy weeks?)

Teaching Aim: To understand how the seventy weeks of Daniel fit into the prophetic scheme.

Outline

1. The Length of the Seventy "Sevens"—9:24a
2. The Purpose of the Seventy "Sevens"—9:24a–f
3. The Three Segments of the Seventy "Sevens"—9:25–26
4. The Cutting Off of the Anointed One—9:26
5. The Covenant Made with Many by the Ruler—9:27

Exegetical Study

Prior to examining this passage of four verses on the seventy "sevens," it is important to notice the twenty-three preceding verses in Daniel 9. In these verses, Daniel's great prayer is answered by God by means of God sending his angel Gabriel to respond. Daniel specifically says that he has been reading the prophecy of Jeremiah (Jer. 25:12; 29:10) about a seventy-year exile. These words had been written by Jeremiah less than a century before Daniel takes to reading them; nevertheless he refers to them as "the Scriptures." Daniel did not wait until the Council of Jamnia in AD 90 pronounced what books were "canonical," for already Jeremiah's book was recognized as one that rightfully belonged in the canon of Scripture. Instead, the canon had always been a matter of "progressive recognition" of those who were closest in time to the writers. Therefore, in less than a hundred years after the book of Jeremiah was composed, Daniel teaches under the inspiration of the Holy Spirit that Jeremiah was part of the Holy Scriptures.

It is out of this conviction that Daniel feels that the period of the seventy-year exile is about to come to an end. In a divine response, Daniel is assured that he is "highly esteemed" (9:23), but that those preceding seventy years of exile will be followed by another period known as the "seventy 'sevens'"; however, it is not stated just how they will relate to those former years, except for the fact that both periods of time share the number "seventy."

1. The Length of the Seventy "Sevens"—9:24a

The angel Gabriel begins his message by saying that "seventy 'sevens'" (NIV; or "seventy weeks," KJV) are "decreed for your people and for your holy city." On the face of it, the word "weeks" or "sevens" could be read as a reference to days, weeks, months, or years. But it is context that is once again determinative, for Daniel had been reading Jeremiah's prophecies (Jer. 25:12; 29:10) that Israel would endure seventy *years* of captivity for violating God's law about allowing the land to rest every seventh year (Lev. 25:1–7). Moreover, 2 Chronicles 36:21 notes that Israel was to be removed from the land so that the land could enjoy seventy years of rest—apparently signifying that Israel had dropped this sabbatical year principle for some 490 years. This would assume that the exile was for seventy years because Israel had missed (i.e., failed to observe) seventy such sabbatical years, that is, sets of seven years! To construe these sevens or weeks as equal to days, or even months, would have shortened the exile, but using that principle of 490 days, or even 490 months, would make both figures fall far short of the actual exile that historically lasted from 605 BC (the year of Daniel's captivity) to 536 BC (the year of Cyrus's decree that the people of Judah could return)—a total of seventy years. Therefore, it seems best to understand these seventy "sevens" or "weeks" as indicating "years."

2. The Purpose of the Seventy "Sevens"—9:24a–f

Verse 24 lists six purposes that the seventy "sevens/weeks" are to accomplish. The first three refer to doing away with transgression, sin, and wickedness. The fourth purpose is "to bring in everlasting righteousness." Thus, it is proper to say that two of the most important elements in the proposed purpose of the seventy sevens is to put an end to sin and to establish everlasting righteousness. Of the six, the third purpose is the clearest and the least debatable: "to atone for wickedness." When the last four purposes are put together, there is a strong case for the prophecy of the seventy sevens running to the very end of the present age, for they speak of a time of purity and righteousness unparalleled in history up to that point.

Some wish to argue that Daniel's prophecy was fulfilled in the first advent of Christ. Accordingly, those who take this position do not agree that the six purposes take us to the end of the present age, and they do not think that the third segment of the seventy weeks involves a prediction of the future work of antichrist in the seventy sevens. It is important that each of the six purposes be examined individually to see what is proposed here.

The first purpose. "To finish transgression" (9:24a). The word "to finish" can also be read "to restrain" transgression. The rendering "to finish" comes from the Hebrew Piel form of the Hebrew verb *kala*, and is what scholars refer to as the *qere*, or what the Masoretes labeled what is "to be read" instead of what is found written in the text. The Masoretes called what is "written" in the text the *kethib*, taken from the same Hebrew verb *katab*, but in a different stem. But both renderings add up to the same meaning, for the word "to restrain" means "a forcible cessation of an activity," such as is seen in Numbers 11:28, where Joshua urged Moses to stop the two elders who continued to prophesy. Joshua wanted Moses to "forbid" them. Thus, in either rendering, it indicates a call for a complete end to all transgression. It is difficult to see how this could happen before the conclusion of the day of the Lord. Moreover, there have been many transgressions and sins that have occurred since the first coming of our Lord, so this prophecy cannot have been fulfilled at the time of the first advent.

The second purpose. "To put an end to sin" (9:24b). Once again, as with the first purpose, there is a difference between what is "written" in the text (the *kethib*) and what is "to be read" (the *qere*). Most commentators take the *qere* reading, which follows the verb *tamam*, meaning, "to bring to an end" or "to complete." If the *kethib* is followed, the Hebrew verb is *khatam*, meaning either "to seal," as one would affix his own seal to a document to authenticate it, or, since the seal came at the end of a document, it was also used to mean "to close" up the document so it would not be seen by anyone else. The first meaning, "to seal" would have no meaning here, therefore if the *kethib* reading is taken, then it must be the second meaning of "seal," which is "bringing to an end." In that case, both purposes are very closely related to one another and refer not to the sins committed up to the time of Christ, but to all sin up to the final day.

The third purpose. "To atone for wickedness" (9:24c). The Hebrew word for "atone" (Hebrew *kafar*) is used often in connection with the sacrificial system in the Old Testament. The KJV translates it "to make atonement" seventy times, and "to reconcile" or "to make reconciliation" only seven times. More accurately, *kafar* means "to ransom or to deliver by [offering] a substitute." Only Messiah can offer pardon for sin, since he offered himself as a vicarious substitute for sin on Calvary.

The fourth purpose. "To bring in everlasting righteousness" (9:24d). This purpose points to a time when the guilt of God's people will be atoned for by the blood of Christ. Some read this purpose as if it said "universal righteousness," which would point to a time when all wickedness is removed from the earth in the reign of Christ. But the phrase reads "everlasting righteousness"; therefore it may be that Daniel avoids the term "universal" so as not to imply that all persons will be made righteous, whether they have put their faith and trust in the coming man of promise, the Messiah, or not.

The fifth purpose. "To seal up vision and prophecy [or prophet]" (9:24e). Once again, the Hebrew word *khatam*, "to seal," has two possible meanings: to seal in the sense of authenticating, i.e., certifying something, or to seal in the sense of closing for the sake of privacy or safekeeping. Again, the choice as to which is the preferred reading is along the lines of one's presuppositions: do these six purposes run only up to Christ's first coming or do they run up to his second coming? Those who take the view of the first advent think that it is contrary to the messianic character of this text to have it run up to the second advent. But when did the term *messianic* refer only to Christ's first coming? The second coming is also equally messianic. Nothing in Scripture says that all messianic texts must be fulfilled in Christ's first coming! Moreover, if the first and second purpose look forward to a complete end to sin's power in this world, then they must extend up to the second coming of Messiah.

The sixth purpose. "To anoint the most holy" (9:24f). The verb "to anoint" is the Hebrew word *mashakh*, from which the word "Messiah" comes as well. It means "to pour oil on something or someone," thereby setting them apart for special service to God.

Each of the six purposes consists of a verb and a noun (or a noun phrase). While the nouns in the first three purposes are all synonyms ("transgression," "sin," "wickedness"), this sixth purpose continues the positive note that the fourth purpose sets forth. The noun phrase literally means a "holy of holies" or the "most holy." But this probably does not mean that part of the temple called the Holy of Holies, for that phrase more frequently appears with an article. Without the article, it can point to the sacrifices, parts of the buildings, lands so designated, or even in a few cases to some person. Yet in some thirty-eight cases where this noun phrase is used, it points to a person only twice (Lev. 27:28; 1 Chron. 23:13).

So the question remains, does this noun phrase "to anoint the most holy" point to Messiah, as Hippolytus and many early commentators argue, or since it is without an article, could it refer to a new temple built after the exile, the establishment of the Christian church, or to a third temple that is yet to be built? There does not appear to be a basis for preferring one view over the other, so it must stand as a mystery for the time being.

3. The Three Segments of the Seventy "Sevens"—9:25–26

At this point, a serious text critical issue must be taken up in the Hebrew Masoretic tradition. While the Masoretic tradition is late (perhaps fourth to sixth century AD) and it may reflect an anti-Christian bias, nevertheless it places the athnak accent (which ordinarily marks the approximate middle of a Hebrew sentence according to the Masoretes) in verse 25 between the "seven weeks" (Hebrew *shabu'im shibah*) and the "sixty-two weeks" (Hebrew *weshabu'im shishim ushenayim*), giving the reading found in the RSV: "from the going forth of the word to restore and build Jerusalem to the coming of the anointed one, a prince, there shall be seven weeks. Then for sixty-two weeks. . . ." This reading differs from the messianic rendering of this passage (e.g., NASB), the final clause of which reads: "there will be seven weeks and sixty-two weeks." On this reading of the text, the sixty-nine weeks (seven + sixty-two) expire before the appearance of the "anointed one," the Messiah, rather than expiring after the seven weeks, as the Masoretic punctuation requires in the alternative reading. There are some early Christian fathers who reflect that Masoretic tradition. For example, Hippolytus supposes that an anointed person appears at the end of the first seven weeks, whom he equates with Joshua the high priest, who is among the returnees from Babylon. Others think this anointed one is Cyrus, who is also called God's "anointed" in Isaiah 45:1.

A reading that seems to be earlier than this fourth- to sixth-century AD Masoretic text, reflected in Theodotion, the Vulgate, and the Syriac versions of the text, combine the seven weeks and the sixty-two weeks to form sixty-nine weeks before the anointed one is "cut off." However, J. Doukhan notes that "where [Theodotion] diverges from the [Masoretic text] [e.g., in the punctuation regarding the counting of the weeks], it is the *only* witness in opposition to the MT [= Masoretic Text]."[2] Moreover, the use of the Hebrew athnak is also difficult to understand unless the solution is that each Hebrew clause is preceded by a waw (= "and"), even when the main verb of the clause occurs later than in the first position in the sentence.

The seventy "weeks," we will then argue, divide into three parts. Verse 25 mentions a segment of seven "sevens/weeks" and another segment of sixty-two "sevens/weeks." The sixty-two "sevens" is mentioned again in verse 26; verse 27 speaks of one "seven/week" along with a "middle to that [one] 'seven.'" So the seventy "sevens/weeks" has three parts to it.

In 1881, Sir Robert Anderson, a gifted Bible scholar who was at the time also the head of Scotland Yard in the United Kingdom, wrote a book titled *The Coming Prince*, in which he argued that the "weeks" here refer to groups of seven years. But he also felt that these years are "prophetic years" of thirty-day months for a total of 360-day years, rather than "solar years" of 365 1/4-day duration. Moreover, he linked the "decree/word" to rebuild the city of Jerusalem with the decree issued by King Artaxerxes Longimanus (Neh. 2:1) as coming on March 14, 445 BC. Therefore, he argued, the seven sevens (forty-nine years) and the sixty-two sevens (434 years), on a 360-day year, yield 173,880 days (483 x 360 days), which would take us to the tenth day of Nisan, April 6, AD 32, Palm Sunday.[3]

Anderson's view is followed by several writers, including Harold W. Hoehner.[4] But there are several problems with this popular view, the most serious being that some doubt there is such a thing as a "prophetic year" of 360 days. The whole argument hinges on whether the numbers given in Noah's flood are meant to be normative for all Scripture, and if the numbers in Revelation 12:6 (42 months = 1,260 days) are meant to be exact or general terms. Nowhere does Scripture claim that in some cases a prophetic year supplants a solar year. Moreover, since Anderson wrote, the dates March 14, 445 BC, and April 6, 32 AD, need to be revised. The first date is now 444 BC, and a 32 AD date for the crucifixion is now untenable and without external verification.[5]

4. The Cutting Off of the Anointed One—9:26

Those who claim the book of Daniel did not record predictions of the future but was written in the Maccabean times hold the view that the one who is "cut off" (9:26) refers to the killing of the innocent high priest Onias in 171 BC. Others say that the "cutting off" refers to the death of our Lord Jesus Christ.

Daniel places this event "after the "sixty-two 'sevens[/weeks]'" (26a). Many interpreters sense that there is a gap between the previous sixty-nine weeks and the final seventieth week, for two things are said to take place: the cutting off of the anointed one [the Messiah], and the destruction of the city and the sanctuary. Since the city and sanctuary in Jerusalem were destroyed by the Romans in AD 70, and the death of the anointed one, who is Christ, occurred around AD 30, this suggests a gap or an interruption in the seventy weeks of some forty years, with no end yet in sight as to how long this gap will continue.

How long this gap lasts is never indicated, but the events that are said to take place in the middle of this week, in verse 27, do not seem to have occurred as of yet, so the gap has extended for some two thousand years to the present moment. Jesus in the Olivet Discourse seems to have put this final week of Daniel at the end of the age, somewhere near the second advent, when he refers to Daniel's "abomination of desolation" (Matt. 24:15). This "anointed one" is also called "a prince" (Hebrew *nagid*) in verse 27.

5. The Covenant Made with Many by the Ruler—9:27

Another ruler will come, who will make a covenant with Israel during this final seventieth week. However, in the middle of that seven-year period of the seventieth "week," he will break his covenant with Israel, just as Antiochus IV Epiphanes did in 167 BC.[6] This ruler, distinct from the anointed Christ, will put an end to sacrifice and offerings. He will, similar to Antiochus Epiphanes, set up "an abomination that causes desolation, until the end that is decreed is poured out on him" (27).

The collapse of the covenant between Israel and this ruler, whom we take to be the antichrist, will unleash a time of unprecedented persecutions, enormous distress, and the horrors of desolations, but it does promise the sixfold blessing as the reason and result of all this coming havoc. It is, of course, important to note that this text addresses or refers to no other group than Daniel and his people Israel. The church does not appear in the discussion of these seventy "sevens."

Conclusions

1. In response to Daniel's prayer as to what happens after the seventy years of exile, which the prophet Jeremiah had predicted, God sent his angel Gabriel to predict another 490 years, a "seventy times seven" for the future of Israel. These 490 years, however, do not occur continuously, but with a significant gap between the sixty-ninth and seventieth weeks.
2. The six purposes divinely ordered for these 490 years cover everything from the final removal of sin to the introduction of "everlasting righteousness" and the sealing up of all visions and prophecies.
3. A gap of an unstated number of years separates the first sixty-nine sevens/weeks from the final week of seven years.
4. In that gap, Messiah is cut off (ca. AD 30) and the city of Jerusalem and the sanctuary are destroyed (AD 70).
5. In the middle of that final set of seven years, the antichrist will break his covenant with Israel and pollute the newly rebuilt third temple with his "abomination that causes desolation."
6. These halcyon years will lead on into the one thousand years of the rule and reign of Christ on earth and then on into eternity and the eternal state.

11

The New Coming Third Temple in Jerusalem

Ezekiel 40:1–41:26; 43:1–11

"This is where I will live among the Israelites forever."

Ezekiel 43:7

One of the most familiar views of Jerusalem is the view from the western slope of the Mount of Olives, where the sun shines on the temple mount's glistening golden Dome of the Rock and silvery roof of Al-Aqsa Mosque, just to the south of the Dome of the Rock. Together, these two Muslim places of worship make up some of the most recognized features of the Holy Land. But what is remarkably absent is any sign of a present Jewish temple structure where the people of Israel have worshiped in the past.

From the early days, when Abraham and his son Isaac went up on that same Mount Moriah (Gen. 22:2; 2 Chron. 3:1) around 2000 BC, this mountain site has been connected with Israel and functioned as the spiritual center on the earth for many. Around 1000 BC, Solomon built the first temple on this same site, which the Babylonians destroyed in 586 BC (Jer. 52:13). Later, a second temple was built, beginning in 520 BC, and dedicated in 516 BC under the prompting of the prophets

111

Haggai and Zechariah and governor Zerubbabel. The Romans reconstructed and enlarged this same second temple over a period of some forty years ending in AD 63, but they destroyed it in AD 70. From that day to this, it has not been rebuilt. What remains is the "Foundation Stone," which, according to the Jewish Mishnah (Yoma 5:2–3), is the spot on the temple mount where God had chosen for the ark of the covenant to rest. According to some it is now the flat bedrock where the small Arab cupola stands in the north portion of the platform, originally called the temple mount. This cupola is known to the Arabs as the "Dome of the Tablets," or the "Dome of the Spirits."

But few things are as dominant in religious Israeli thought as the need for a third temple to be built in the last days, especially since it is to be available for the time when the Messiah returns in his second advent. For example, in a recent poll conducted by the Panels Institute in Israel, almost two-thirds of today's Jewish people said they want to see such a temple built again, a number which included 47 percent who regard themselves as secular Jews![1] Attention to this fact is heightened annually in the observance of *Tisha B'av*, on the ninth day of the month Av, which in 2009 corresponded to July 30. This Jewish holiday marks the destruction of the first and second temples, both of which were destroyed on exactly the same day, though in years widely spread apart (586 BC and AD 70). It is traditionally a day of great mourning, particularly for religious Jews.

In connection with this day, a group formed over fifty years ago by Gershom Salomon, called "The Temple Mount Faithful," has annually attempted to haul a four-and-a-half-ton cornerstone (which they hope will be the start of the third temple) up the temple mount, but they have been stopped each year by the local police, as well as Israel's Supreme Court.

Nevertheless, the hope that the temple in Jerusalem will one day be rebuilt has never been abandoned, for the daily synagogue prayers also keep it alive. In that prayer, known as the prayer of the "Eighteen Benedictions," called "*Shmoneh Esre*," the eighteenth benediction begins, "Be pleased, Lord our God, with thy people Israel and with their prayer; restore the worship of thy most holy sanctuary."[2] That prayer has daily been on the lips of Jewish people for over two thousand years, but especially since AD 691 when the Muslims built the Dome of the Rock on that same temple platform.

On one recent day, it seemed as if that prayer would suddenly be answered. On June 7, 1967, Israeli troops moved into the Old City of Jerusalem during the Six-Day War, and some Jewish paratroopers occupied the temple mount as the Israeli military dropped down on the temple platform and flew the Israeli flag over that area which had been under Muslim control since AD 691. However, Moshe Dayan, the Israeli defense minister, had the flag taken down after ten days and returned the temple mount back to Muslim control once again. So great was the potential for conflict with Islam that for the moment it became more of a political liability than an asset for Israel to keep possession of the former temple mount.

So exciting had been Israel's conquest of Jerusalem and the temple mount that *Time* magazine ran a headline article in its June 20, 1967, issue following the capture of the temple mount. The article said, "Assuming that Israel keeps the [Western] Wall [indeed, it has], which is one of few remaining ruins of Judaism's second temple, has the time come for the erection of the Third Temple?" The article went on to contend that Israel's euphoria was so great over this conquest that many believed Israel had already entered the messianic era, when such a building would occur.

More recently the Israel News Service (INS), for March 2, 1998, ran this headline: "Children wanted for Future Temple service. Ultra-orthodox Jewish sect is searching for parents willing to hand over newborn sons to be raised in isolation and purity in preparation for the rebuilding of the biblical temple in Jerusalem. Only members of the Jewish priestly caste, the Kohanim, need apply."

Another rabbi, Rabbi Yisrael Ariel, founded the "Temple Institute" in 1987. He was one of the first Israeli paratroopers to reach the temple mount during that same Six-Day War in 1967. He has wanted to start the preparation for the third temple and the arrival of Messiah by getting the temple utensils crafted and ready for use. Not far from the Western Wall, Ariel and his team conduct meticulous research on the appearance, size, and function of these sacred vessels and implements to be used in the temple. Ariel's team is rebuilding these implements, using gold, silver, copper, and wood for their materials, often placing many of these completed items on display at their headquarters.

In the meantime, a search goes on for the ark of the covenant, which is by far the most important item in the temple itself. So sacred is the ark that any improper handling of it had in the past resulted in death (1 Sam. 6:19; 1 Chron. 13:9–10). The last time the ark was seen was in 2 Chronicles 8:11, where King Solomon asked his wife, the daughter of pagan Pharaoh, to leave the area where the ark was kept and reside in her own home southeast of the temple mount. The ark was lost sometime after that and has not reappeared since then.

Stories exist that claim the ark of the covenant was taken to Ethiopia by Prince Menelik I of Ethiopia, allegedly the son of the Queen of Sheba and the illegitimate offspring of King Solomon, but no positive proof yet exists to confirm this popular story, despite its repetition in the *Encyclopedia Britannica*. Others say it is hidden under the temple mount in the labyrinth of catacombs. However, others note that Jeremiah 3:16 teaches that "in those days . . . 'the ark of the covenant of the LORD' . . . will never enter their minds or be remembered; it will not be missed, nor will another one be made." So the question is, which of these scenarios is correct on the matter of the ark of the covenant?

Such talk inevitably brings up the question as to how Israel would go about replacing, if that is what it will take, the Dome of the Rock and Al-Aqsa, which currently occupy this platform. The beautiful Dome of the Rock was erected by Caliph Abdel Malik on the temple mount in AD 691. For over thirteen centuries, many have believed that the Dome of the Rock was built directly over where the original temple stood. But that is now shown to be incorrect.

In the months that followed the recapture of the temple mount in June of 1967, Israeli archaeologists began to dig a 900-foot long tunnel in a northerly direction along the face of the Western Wall of the temple platform, starting from the spot known as Wilson's Arch. This tunnel is almost 200 feet below the present level of the streets of Jerusalem. It has become known as the "Rabbi's Tunnel," because the Rabbis used it to approach as closely as they dared to the site of the Holy of Holies without stepping on that holy ground. Currently, religious Israelis are forbidden to go up on the temple mount for fear they might accidentally step on the spot where the Holy of Holies originally stood.

The Rabbi's Tunnel, however, was able to expose the original massive Herodian foundation stones of the temple mount, some probably weighing up to four hundred tons, measuring up to 46 feet by 10 feet by 10 feet. However, the prize-find came several hundred feet north of Wilson's Arch, where a gate was uncovered that originally led to the temple mount from the west in the time of the second temple. This Herodian Western Gate was directly opposite the Eastern (Golden) Gate across the platform, just as the Mishnah had recorded. This meant that the Dome of the Rock was built some 150 feet south of the original site of the temple, which was directly west of the Eastern Gate.

A further confirmation of this new identification for the original site of the second temple is the location of the small Arabic cupola that lies north of the Dome of the Rock in a large open space, and on a straight line from the middle of the Eastern Gate to the opposite side of the mount at the Western Gate. This cupola is known in Arabic as *Qubbat el-Arwah*, the "Dome of the Spirits" (or winds), which stands, it would appear, by itself over the bedrock of Mount Moriah. This site is also called *Qubbat el-Alouah*, the "Dome of the Tablets." The Jewish Mishnah notes that there was a foundation stone in the temple known as the *"Eben Shetiyah,"* a foundation stone on which the ark of the covenant rested.

The interesting result of all of these data is that the temple could conceivably be rebuilt on the original temple platform without necessarily disrupting the Dome of the Rock or the Al-Aqsa Mosque. Whether some sort of peace accord will eventually make this possible by means of a new round of religious-pluralism negotiation that allows the two religions to exist side by side, or a covenant agreement with the antichrist that gives a little bit to everyone in the Israeli-Arab conflict, is still very speculative. But such an agreement and such a location of a third temple would not need to call for a destruction of those two sacred places in the Muslim world. But this too is very speculative and does not face up to all of the current realities.

For many gentile believers, the building of a third temple is still a very difficult prospect to even envisage, much less to conceive as part of God's plan for the future. Few passages of the Bible appear to be more puzzling and less read, much less preached on, than Ezekiel 40–48. However, the prophet Ezekiel had a vision of a man with a measuring line, who measured the dimensions of a temple, whose dimensions have never been realized thus far in space and time in either the first or second temple. If these chapters, with all their specific measurements, are to be taken realistically and naturally, which we think is the most probable interpretation of these texts, then there must be a third temple that is still to come.

The New Coming Third Temple

Text: Ezekiel 40:1–41:26; 43:1–11
Title: "The New Coming Third Temple"

Focal Point: Ezekiel 43:7, "Son of man, this is the place of my throne and the place for the soles of my feet. This is where I will live among the Israelites forever."

Homiletical Keyword: Anticipations

Interrogative: What? (What are the anticipations we can have for the building of the third temple in Israel?)

Teaching Aim: To show that God will direct a third temple to be built, which will open up the possibility for the events connected with the second coming of our Lord.

Outline

1. A Vision of a New Structure—40:1–4
2. A Vision of a New Outer Court for the Temple—40:5–27
3. A Vision of a New Inner Court of the Temple—40:28–47
4. The New Third Temple of the Lord—40:48–41:26
5. God's Return to the Temple—43:1–11

Introduction

Few chapters of the Bible separate interpreters into such strongly diverse camps of interpretation as the last nine chapters of Ezekiel—probably more than at any other place in the Scriptures. The literal method of interpreting the Bible seems to be miles away from those who spiritualize or allegorize these texts. Even more distressing is the fact that even within the camps of the amillennialists and the premillennialists, there often is very little homogeneity.

Some Christian interpreters believe the temple described in these texts of Ezekiel is a literal temple that will be built toward the end of the days on earth connected in general with the return of the Lord. But the sacrifices and the priesthood in the texts must be cared for interpretively by something other than a literal interpretation, since Christ has by his death and resurrection put away the sacrifice for sin once and for all (Heb. 9:11–15; 10:1–4, 18). Therefore, they say that these ritual acts are either done as a memorial of what Christ has done definitively or they function as a way of speaking of worship in the future under the rubrics of worship in the past. However, it is difficult to see how the ancient forms of worship could be a memorial of what the Messiah did on the cross, since the Messiah himself will be present at that time. A memorial of his work would seem to be somewhat inappropriate given his presence. Nevertheless, the point is well taken, and this aspect of the text is puzzling to say the least.

Exegetical Study

1. A Vision of a New Structure—40:1–4

Just as the prophet's ministry began in chapters 1–3 with a great vision, so he ends the last section of his prophecy with another vision with breathtaking detail. In fact, there is a formal introduction in 40:1–4 that forms a convincing inclusio with 43:10–11. These two sections appear to be crafted so as to have the conclusion in 43:10–11 answer the introduction found in 40:1–4.

The date line in Ezekiel 40:1 points back to Ezekiel 1:1 and 33:21. It is now twenty-five years since Ezekiel had been taken captive by Nebuchadnezzar (ca. 597 BC), and fourteen years since the fall of Jerusalem in 586 BC as mentioned in this book (1:1). Thus the time is about the year of 573 BC. Furthermore, the date can be set even more exactly: "the tenth day of the month at the beginning of the year" (40:1). Thus, as the Jewish New Year's Day came in the spring in the month of Nisan, on the tenth day, that tenth day in that month computes to our calendars as April 28, 573 BC.

God's hand is upon the prophet once again as he is transported in a vision "to the land of Israel" where God "set [him] on a very high mountain, on whose south side were some buildings that looked like a city" (2). Neither the city nor the mountain is here named, but this may be because of the prophet's continuing polemic against that city and nation because of its wickedness.

The instrument the attending angel uses to measure the various parts of the coming temple[3] is a line of flax that functions as a sort of tape measure. Presumably it is a long ropelike affair that has knots tied off for every cubit. The angel also has a measuring rod that functions as a long yardstick. As he lays it down, Ezekiel calls out the rods (or reeds). Since Ezekiel is writing from Babylon, he no doubt uses the long Babylonian cubit, which is 21 inches long. The six-cubit-long measuring rod with six "handbreadths" is taken to be 10 1/2 feet long in our Western measurements.

But why is all this detail included? It is because Ezekiel was to present a message of hope to those in the Babylonian captivity (Ezek. 40:4; 43:10–12). For those who are still in shock over the burning of the first temple, God tells of a time when he will restore his own messianic temple. The people then had best get ready for the coming of Messiah and his future kingdom.

2. A Vision of a New Outer Court for the Temple—40:5–27

As with all of Israel's temples, this future temple is surrounded by a wall. This wall is 10 1/2 feet high and 10 1/2 feet broad, enclosing a temple area of nearly three football fields, measuring 875 feet by 875 feet.

The eastern gate (6–16) is the most significant gate theologically and also architecturally, for it serves as the basis for describing all the other gates, which have the identical measurements. It also is the gate through which the Messiah himself will enter.

The wall of the eastern gate is as thick as the walls surrounding the temple area. First, one has to climb a set of seven steps before one enters a small room 10 1/2 feet square. In fact, there are six such rooms in the gate area, all identical in size and each divided by a wall. Each chamber has two narrow windows similar to the slits used in ancient castles. The entrances to each of these gate chambers are ornamented with the image of palm trees.

Before exiting the gate building and entering the outer court, the prophet Ezekiel stands in a porch area some 14 feet long. Altogether, the whole gate building measures almost 44 feet wide and 87 1/2 feet long.

Once the prophet is through the eastern gate, the angel escorts him around the outer court of the temple (17–27). He observes a pavement on the east, north, and south side of the temple area covered in mosaic tile, which is slightly lower in elevation than the chambers around it. Within this court, the prophet sees ten open chambers located on the north, south, and east walls, making thirty in all. Neither we nor the prophet are told what purpose these chambers serve. Later, however, in Ezekiel 46:19–24, we are informed that in all four corners of the temple there are small courtyards that house kitchens for the preparation of sacrifices the people will bring.

3. A Vision of a New Inner Court of the Temple—40:28–47

Both a north and a south gate give access to the inner court of the temple by ascending eight steps. These two gates are made exactly like the gates that give access to the outer court, except these inner gateways have four small tables, two on each side of the gateway (38–41), to be used for the preparation of the sacrifices. These tables are made of dressed stone, and on them are the utensils for slaughtering the burnt offerings. The tables have rings on their sides. On the wall all around are double-pronged hooks, each about 3 inches long.

The traffic pattern for the people makes a way for entering from the north gate and exiting at the south gate, but the eastern gate is exclusively for the prince (Ezek. 44:1–3). This eastern gate is open for the public only on holidays.

The inner court (40:44–47) is 175 feet by 175 feet. In this inner court, by the north gateway, is a chamber facing south and designated for the singers (44). Another similar chamber is by the side of the south gateway into the inner court facing north, but this one is for the priests who have charge of the altar, while the one facing south is for the priests who have charge of the temple.

4. The New Third Temple of the Lord—40:48–41:26

Just as the previous two temples were set on a platform, so this future temple is set on a platform of 10 1/2 feet, high with a flight of stairs leading up into the temple. At the top of the stairs on this platform are two large bronze pillars at the entrance, just as Solomon's and later Herod's temple. After passing the pillars, one enters a vestibule, and then one enters large, ornately carved bifold doors leading into the temple.

Once inside the temple, the Holy Place measures 70 feet long by 35 feet wide. The walls are paneled with wood and ornate carvings of palm trees and cherubs alternating around the room. Each cherub has two faces: a man's face and a young lion's face (41:18–19).

The next room is the Holy of Holies, which is entered by a door similar to the one Ezekiel used to enter the Holy Place. Ezekiel does not enter the Holy of Holies, but he is told by the angel that the room is 35 feet square. Missing are the old veil that separated the two rooms and the ark of the covenant. No mention is made of either piece that was in temples one and two.

Ezekiel is then taken outside the temple where he observes a number of chambers along the three exterior walls—the north, south, and west walls, but not the east wall (41:11). There are thirty chambers along the three walls reaching three stories high, making ninety chambers in all, perhaps intended as priests' quarters and storage units.

Along the far west area of the temple is a place separated from the temple called the *gizrah*, from the verbal root meaning "to cut off" or "to separate from" (41:12–15). Whether this space is as a storage area for things that are not ritually clean, or whether it is for items used in the maintenance of the temple area, we do not know.

More detail on the third temple is provided in the text following our key passage, such as the priests' chambers, which are defined in Ezekiel 42:1–14, followed by the description of the altar in 43:13–27, and the kitchens in 46:19–24. But best of all is the fact that this is a place called "The LORD is there" (48:35), *Yahweh Shammah*. It is the presence of the Lord that makes this temple so significant!

5. God's Return to the Temple—43:1–11

As a climactic event to the building project, therefore, the prophet Ezekiel describes the return of the glory of the Lord. In it, Ezekiel portrays the temple itself, rather than the ark of the covenant, as the throne of the Lord. This departs from the inaugural vision in Ezekiel 1:24–28, where the cherubim carry the throne of God. Here there is a silence about the cherubim or even the ark of the covenant.

The glory of the Lord that earlier moves from above the cherubim in the Holy of Holies to the threshold of the temple (10:4), stopping at the east gate to the Lord's house (10:19), stopping at the Mount of Olives, east of Jerusalem (11:23), and then departing from the area is now seen in Ezekiel 43:2 as coming from the east and once again filling the temple (43:4). For all those who had seen or heard of the catastrophic effects of the departure of the glory of God from his temple and his city of Jerusalem prior to the 586 BC sack of Jerusalem and the temple, here is a new sign of real hope for the future.

In light of the reappearance of the glory of the Lord, the Israelites are challenged to relinquish their spiritual harlotry and their pagan funerary practices. Only then will Yahweh establish permanent residence in the midst of his people, for he is holy and separate from all sin and unrighteousness.

Conclusions

1. Not everyone understands this vision of Ezekiel in the same way as we have traced it here, but there is no doubt that the detail given here amounts to more than a symbol or an allegory

of the Christian church. It would take an enormous amount of allegorizing to satisfy the plethora of detail and exactness of description of this temple.

2. Taken at face value, these chapters in Ezekiel depict a literal third temple that will be built in Jerusalem and used during the millennium when Jesus Christ reigns on this earth (Isa. 2:3; 60:13; Jer. 33:18; Joel 3:18; Mic. 4:2; Zech. 14:16, 20–21).

3. Most significant of all is the fact that the Lord himself will be present and reside in his temple on earth.

12

The Coming Antichrist

Daniel 11:36–45

"He will exalt and magnify himself above every god."
Daniel 11:36

World history has had more than its share of dictators and national leaders who aspired to having the whole world at their feet. Each aspirant has come and gone, whether it be the ancient Pharaohs, an Assyrian Shalmanezer, a Babylonian Nebuchadnezzar, a Greek Alexander the Great, the Roman Ceasars, the French Napoleon, the German Hitler, an Iraqi Sadam Hussein, an Iranian Ayatollah Khomeini, or an Ahmadinejad. But a new tool was placed in the hands of aspirants to the title of world dictator at the end of World War II, demonstrated by an atomic holocaust unleashed by the United States against Hiroshima and Nagasaki, Japan. From that time onward, with the development of missiles armed with nuclear warheads, most of the world's cities were often within approximately thirty minutes of complete destruction by a dictator who could press a button at distances halfway around the globe, or from missiles on board a container ship located off the shores of the continents of the world!

But who would use such a massive tool for destruction? Where would such a ruler come from? Does Scripture give any hint as to his origins and motives? Would he be successful, and is this old globe headed for trouble such as we have never seen before at the hands of such a megalomaniac?

As far back as the days of the prophet Daniel in the fifth century BC, God predicted that only four world empires would appear in world history: the Babylonian Empire, the Medo-Persian Empire, the Greco-Macedonian Empire, and the Roman Empire (Dan. 2:31–44; 7:17–27). It is amazing that throughout history, even though a number of ambitious men would attempt to replace the Roman Empire with their own fifth empire, none would ever succeed. Some of those who tried their best were Muhammad, Charlemagne, Genghis Khan, Napoleon, the British (where the sun never sets on the "Union Jack"), Adolph Hitler, and the Russians, but all eventually fell (or will fall) far short of having a world empire over which they ruled.

However, the fourth empire mentioned in the book of Daniel, the Roman Empire, decreed by God to experience a revival in the last days of earth's history, in which a confederacy of ten nations, apparently mostly in the Mediterranean basin and in the old territory occupied by the former Roman Empire (Dan. 7:7–8), will arise. This will be a further manifestation of the fourth part of the image of Daniel 2:31–34 and the fourth beast of Daniel 7:7–8. The image of Daniel 2 is pictured as having legs of iron and clay, while the beast of Daniel 7 is "terrifying and frightening and very powerful," with "large iron teeth," that devours or stamps on all that is in sight.

This fourth empire consists of ten horns, or ten kings, who will see three of the ten horns defeated, as another horn, "the little horn," takes over as the new leader of the western forces. This new leader, later known as the antichrist, will demonstrate absolute power, until he is destroyed by Messiah in the battle of Armageddon.

"The Ancient of Days . . . gave [Daniel] this explanation" regarding the symbols used here:

> The fourth beast is a fourth kingdom that will appear on earth. It will be different from all the other kingdoms and will devour the whole earth, tramping it down and crushing it. The ten horns are ten kings who will come from this kingdom. After them another king will arise, different from the earlier ones; he will subdue three kings. He will speak against the Most High and oppress his saints and try to change the set times and the laws. The saints will be handed over to him for a time, times and half a time. (Dan. 7:22–25)

The revival of the old Roman Empire will approximate, so it would seem, the same geographical outlines set by the earlier Roman Empire. This process may well have started, some think, in 1958 with the founding of the European Common Market, officially known as the European Economic Community, or the EEC, and the North Atlantic Treaty Organization, or NATO. These nations may have unknowingly taken the first tentative steps toward what Daniel had predicted as the coming ten horns, or ten-nation confederation. It is of more than passing interest that the EEC is based on the "Treaty of Rome," which was signed in Rome on March 25, 1967. It was said by one of the architects of this treaty, Jean Monnet, that ultimately, "Once a Common Market interest [has] been created, then political union will come naturally." It appears, then, that these embryonic moves will provide for future political unions along with the current economic, defense, and customs provisions.

The term "antichrist," of course, does not appear in the Old Testament, but arises with the apostle John in his writings in 1 John 2:18, 22; 4:3; and 2 John 7. Nevertheless, both testaments are filled with descriptive epithets for this coming person: he is called "a little horn" (Dan. 7:8), "a stern-faced king" (Dan. 8:23), "the ruler who will come" (Dan. 9:26), the one who "causes desolation" (Dan. 9:27), "a contemptible person" (Dan. 11:21), "the king [who] will do as he pleases" (Dan. 11:36), "the worthless shepherd" (Zech. 11:17), "the man of lawlessness" (2 Thess. 2:3), "the lawless one" (2 Thess. 2:8), and "the beast" (Rev. 11:7; 13:1; 14:9; 15:2; 16:2; 17:3, 13; 19:20; 20:10). Since the apostle John proclaimed that there would be many antichrists (1 John 2:18), the personage of the antichrist was progressively revealed through a series of opponents of the Jewish people and in particular those who would desecrate Jerusalem and the temple of the Lord.

I have chosen Daniel 11:36–45, the single most extensive teaching passage in the Old Testament on the character and the rise of the antichrist, from which to draw our teaching or expository preaching on this theme. It is to this passage, then, that we now turn.

The Antichrist as Head of the Revived Roman Empire

Text: Daniel 11:36–45

Title: "The Antichrist as Head of the Revived Roman Empire"

Focal Point: Daniel 11:36, "The king will do as he pleases. He will exalt and magnify himself above every god and will say unheard-of things against the God of gods. He will be successful until the time of wrath is completed, for what has been determined must take place."

Homiletical Keyword: Characteristics

Interrogative: What? (What are the characteristics of antichrist that should warn us about the future?)

Teaching Aim: To make us aware that there is coming a final world ruler out of the ruins of the old Roman Empire who will seem overwhelmingly successful until the Lord puts a full stop to his global ambitions and outrages.

Outline

1. The Ungodly Character of Antichrist—11:36–39
2. The Battles and Sure End of Antichrist—11:40–45

Exegetical Study

1. The Ungodly Character of Antichrist—11:36–39

Not all Bible expositors agree on the identity of "the king" in Daniel 11:36–45. They are divided between his being the historical Antiochus IV Epiphanes (215–163 BC) or confining his identity to being equated with the future antichrist. Certainly in favor of the Antiochus Epiphanes view is the fact that there seems to be no indication given of a sudden switch in topics in verse 36 from its contemporary context.

Antiochus is one of those forerunners of the coming antichrist as judged by his description. However, in favor of a heightened view that sees the antichrist himself in verse 36 are the following arguments. First of all, Antiochus is never referred to with the article as "the king," even though he (and his predecessors) was labeled as the "king of the North" (11:6). Moreover, this one called "the king" is set over against another called "the king of the South," whom "the king" will oppose in Daniel 11:40. Second, the character and policies of "the king" in Daniel 11:36–39 are strange if they are here, at his late stage, being introduced to explain who Antiochus is, after we have had him and his work already presented in this context. Third, numerous details are set forth in verses 40–45 that do not match the era or events in the life of Antiochus. Fourth, Antiochus is presented three times previously in the book of Daniel, but he is only called "king" once in Daniel 11:27, along with Ptolemy.

Therefore, "the king" in verse 36 is best viewed as the coming head of the revived Roman Empire, the antichrist. He is referred to as being a willful king who does "as he pleases" (36a). In this regard, the final antichrist shares the same insolent, self-centered attitude, which demanded everything be done the way he wanted it done, as his forerunner, Antiochus IV Epiphanes. But the insolence and self-willed arrogance predicted of the coming antichrist in Daniel 7:25 and 8:24 (and later in Rev. 13:7; 17:13) exceeded the impudence shown already in history by Antiochus IV.

In proof of his outrageous character, the antichrist will "exalt and magnify himself above every god" (36b). Not only will he exalt himself above all people, but in self-deification, he will magnify himself even above God. That is why he will "speak against the Most High" (7:25; cf. 2 Thess. 2:4). Even though he will worship the gods of Greece and demand that the Jews do the same, he will nevertheless set himself above every other god and even blaspheme God's name (Rev. 13:6), as he will attempt to change the laws of God (Dan. 7:25). He will also "say unheard-of things against the God of gods" (11:36c). The word translated by the NIV as "unheard-of things" is the Hebrew word *pala'*, meaning in the Hebrew plural Niphal stem participle, "things that are amazing, marvelous, [or] dreadful." Surely these things will be astonishing and unbelievable, so unique will they be. But with lots of chutzpah, he will dare to speak against God in a way that will be different and to a degree that few, if any others, have been emboldened to try.

Amazingly, antichrist "will be successful until the time of wrath is completed" (36d). The word used for "the time of wrath" (Hebrew *za'am*), also rendered "[the] indignation" (RSV) or the "appointed time of the end" (NASB) in Daniel 8:19, is a reference to the seventieth week of Daniel, otherwise known as the seven years, or the final years of tribulation that were predicted would happen to Daniel and his people Israel, when the antichrist would with all his might attack nations and Israel up until his demise at the end of the seven years (9:27). That end for him "ha[d already] been determined" to "take place" (11:36e).

In three separate areas will the antichrist "show no regard," "understanding," or "pleasure":

1. this man will show no regard for the "gods of his fathers,"
2. nor will he have any "desire of women," and
3. he will have no place for "any god" (37).

Accordingly, none of these matters will move him, for his heritage and cultural upbringing will be worth nothing to him. His inhumanity and unnatural attitude to women continues the ancient enmity of Satan himself toward all womanhood. Nor will deities matter at all to him; he will be more interested in his own deity.

In place of all these traditional loyalties, and particularly "any god" (if that is the correct antecedent of "instead of them" [38a]), he will honor a "god of fortresses" (38b). The word for "fortresses" is used in Daniel 11 six other times (1, 7, 10, 19, 31, 39), each of them signaling a "strong place." Therefore, it is not that his god is mighty and powerful, for he despises allegiance to any god, but rather his god is his own military programs, his strongholds, and his fortresses. As such, he will honor "a god unknown to his fathers" (38c). The earlier Roman Empire had placed a heavy emphasis on her gods and religious activity, but this leader of a future revived Roman Empire will deny all worship and honoring of deities and place his emphasis instead on military activity. Instead of honoring the old deities, as the earlier Romans did, with "gold and silver and costly gifts/precious stones" (38c–d), he will see that gold, silver, and "desirable things" are spent on warfare, military hardware, and armaments.

With a bold audacity, antichrist will not hold back from attacking any stronghold, and the satanically aided ruler will appear to be invincible. The reference to the "help of a foreign[/strange] god" (39a) is not explained, but given his antipathy for all deities, one wonders if this could be a reference to Satan himself.

Those whom the antichrist will conquer and who will "acknowledge him" (39b), antichrist will "make . . . rulers over many people and [will] distribute the land at a price" (39c–d). They will be given positions of leadership in his own government or made subrulers over conquered territories. The amount of territory ceded to them will depend, apparently, on the degree of obedience they render to him and the subruler's potential of help in the cause of antichrist.

2. The Battles and Sure End of Antichrist—11:40–45

The second half of this teaching passage on the antichrist deals with his wars against the ten kings in the middle of the tribulation (40–45). It is said to be "at the time of the end" (40), which is continued in Daniel 12:1 as "at that time," where Daniel immediately gives three of the most important events in the eschatological calendar of the end of days: the great tribulation of Israel, the resurrection of the dead, and the final reward of the righteous (12:1–3). The previous time notice of "until the time of wrath[/indignation]" (11:36) is now sharpened as "in [literally, the Hebrew preposition *be*-] the time of the end" (40). If the time we are speaking of is the time of the great tribulation, otherwise known as the seventieth week of Daniel, then the reference is to the days of the tribulation, the final seven years mentioned earlier by Daniel in chapter 9.

The antichrist will move out in all directions as he succeeds in killing three kings (cf. Dan. 7:8–20, 24): the king of the north (perhaps Syria), the king of the south (Egypt), and the king of the east (which may be the same as the horde of 200 million soldiers arriving from the east, cf. Rev. 9:16; 16:12).

The king of the south is the easier identification, for it refers to Egypt's leader as an officer of the Arab world. This ruler shall "push" (i.e., "push like a goat," Dan. 8:4) at the antichrist to stop him in his dreams of the world empire, but it will be to no effect. He will be defeated.

The king of the north seems to qualify as the successor of the line of the Seleucids, but given our present history, that does not appear very likely to many interpreters. They opt instead for the present nation of Russia, but if the battle of Gog and Magog has just preceded this build-up to Armageddon (and preceded the seven years of the great tribulation), how could the Russian leader have rebounded so quickly? Neither can the king of the north be a reference to the antichrist, for never in the previous contexts in Daniel has he ever been referred to as such. The base of antichrist's power will be Rome and not Syria. Even though Moscow is almost on a direct north-south line with Jerusalem, as such he might be seen as the king of the north, but this does not allow for the impact of Ezekiel 38–39, with its staggering military loss of life and the huge loss of face to be factored in if the battle of Gog and Magog is correctly located as one that precedes this battle near the beginning, or just before, the tribulation period.

Antichrist's conquest of Egypt will open up the way for his conquest of Africa (11:42–43). Thus the Nubians and the Libyans will submit to him as the treasures of Egypt's silver and gold flow into his coffers. These will be just part of the numerous invasions he will conduct as he sweeps through these lands "like a flood" (40).

The weapons listed in verse 40, "chariots and cavalry and a great fleet of ships," may only be representative of their counterparts in modern warfare, but they may also be a return to some aspects of older methods of fighting for reasons that will be obvious in that day. For instance, Russia still maintains one of the largest cavalry units found in any major country. Could this also be true in the future of other countries?

But the most astounding fact in this list of military objectives comes in verse 41: "he [the antichrist] will also invade the Beautiful Land." After antichrist has triumphed over the king of the north and the king of the south, he will move into the "[Glorious/]Beautiful Land," which is Israel/Palestine, as the same phrase indicates in 11:16 and 8:9. There is no mention of where this battle will be located, but if this is the climactic battle of Armageddon, as Revelation 16:16 records it, this battle is the same one described in Zechariah 14:2, which climaxes in the fall of Jerusalem.

The "many" (11:41) that "will fall" must be Jewish people (not "countries" as supplied by NIV), since it is now about the middle of the seventieth week of the seven years of tribulation when antichrist will break his infamous "covenant" with the Jews (Dan. 9:27). Now as supreme master of a good part of the world, he will be in the driver's seat to force his will wherever and however he wishes. Given his irreligious stance, the Jews with their revived worship of God at the third temple in Jerusalem will no doubt be a source of irritation to him. Moreover, the land of Israel, a long-standing prize of the nations, will be a particularly important feather in his cap. No doubt Satan will influence him to break his covenant with Israel, thereby forcing the cessation of all services in this new temple as he erects his "abomination that causes desolation" in that same temple (9:27), imitating his forerunner Antiochus Epiphanes.

The former nations of Edom, Moab, and the leaders of Ammon, which today make up the modern state of Jordan, where many Jews will have fled for refuge, will not be invaded for some reason (11:41).

While the antichrist is in Africa, he will receive "reports from the east and the north" (44). What these reports or rumors are about is not communicated here, but they will be enough to cause him enormous alarm. One guess is that he will suddenly hear of a movement of 200 million troops from the east (Rev. 9:16; 16:12), along with others from the north. This will cause antichrist to return to Israel to remedy the situation. In his enormous rage, he will set out to destroy and annihilate "many." This may be the time when "two-thirds" of the land of Israel will perish (Zech. 13:8), leaving only one-third left in the land of Israel!

The passage concludes with a description of where antichrist will set up his new headquarters. Antichrist will set up his palatial royal tents as ancient conquerors did at the place of their encampments (Dan. 11:45). A large tent was usually pitched for the king, and smaller ones were pitched around it for his personal attendants. The "tent" then became a symbol of both his base of operations and his domination over the land.

The place he will choose to locate his tent will be between the seas, between the Mediterranean Sea and the Dead Sea. But more particularly, his tent will be "at the beautiful mountain" (45). This means no less than in Jerusalem on Mount Zion. By now, antichrist has reached the zenith of his power as Israel lies prostrate at his feet in an appalling desolation. This terrible state of affairs is described in more detail in Revelation 19:11–21.

"Yet he will come to his end, and no one will help him" (Dan. 11:45). Christ himself will come in all his power against antichrist and his army, as they meet in the Valley of Jehoshaphat (Joel 3:2, 12), east of Jerusalem. The only help left to antichrist, as he has alienated every other nation, will be his chief helper, the false prophet. But this false prophet, along with antichrist and his army, will at this point be cast into the lake of fire, as they are consumed by the "sword" that proceeds out of the mouth of Christ (Rev. 19:15). So much for the world's final world conqueror!

Conclusions

1. Antichrist is the final world ruler who opposes God and his Messiah as he seeks to usurp the place of divine worship by his desecration of the temple in Jerusalem.
2. His personage reflects the spirit of the age, which will be anti-theocratic, anti-Semitic, and antibiblical in every way possible.
3. Just as many of antichrist's forerunners will exhibit negative aspects of his characteristics, the antichrist himself will be one mean dude who is as self-willed and self-exalting as this world has ever seen.
4. Christ will come a second time and not only end this man's career and his army, but will set up his own righteous government and reign for the next one thousand years.

13

The Battle of Armageddon

Zechariah 14:1–21

"The LORD will be king over the whole earth."

Zechariah 14:9

The final six chapters of Zechariah focus on the overthrow of all world powers and the establishment of Messiah's rule into eternity after his thousand-year rule on the earth. The first three of the final six chapters of Zechariah 9–14, chapters 9–11, deal with the way God will bring the gentile powers to an end and the way Israel will be endowed with power to overcome all her enemies. But the last three chapters of this book, chapters 12–14, deal with the way Israel herself will be sifted and purged by the final conflict with all the nations of the world. Thus, whereas Zechariah 9–11 features the victories of Alexander the Great leading up to Messiah's first advent, chapters 12–14 go on to a more distant time and the events surrounding the second coming of our Lord Jesus Christ.

Few places in the Bible show more dramatically the absurdities of an allegorizing type of interpretation than the passage before us. For example, if we say allegorically, or in a spiritualizing mode of interpretation, that "Israel" in this passage does not speak of a real ethnopolitical entity called Israel, but instead figuratively of the Christian church, then when Zechariah 13:8 says that "two-thirds will be struck down and perish," it would have to mean that "two-thirds" of the church will be killed in this event. Since Zechariah 14 is but an enlargement on Zechariah 13:9, it is important that the identity of "Israel" in the text be maintained as being a real geo-political nation and the ethnically real Jewish people of Israel.

Preparing for God's Glorious Consummation of History at Armageddon

Text: Zechariah 14:1–21

Title: "Preparing for God's Glorious Consummation of History at Armageddon"

Focal Point: Verse 9, "The LORD will be king over the whole earth. On that day there will be one LORD, and his name the only name."

Homiletical Keyword: Events

Interrogative: What? (What events will God use to conclude human history?)

Teaching Aim: To show that the battle of Armageddon is earth's final attempt to overthrow the kingdom of God and the people of God, as set forth in the promise-plan of God.

Outline

1. Our Nations Will Fight Jerusalem for the Last Time—14:1–3
   1.1. The Siege of Jerusalem—14:1
   1.2. The Success of the Nations—14:2
   1.3. A Deliverer Shall Save the Remnant—14:3
2. Our Messiah Will Appear a Second Time on Earth—14:4–7
3. Our Messiah's Kingdom Will Be Established over All—4:8–15
   3.1. It Will Issue Living Waters—14:8
   3.2. The Lord Will Be Sovereign—14:9
   3.3. Peace Will Never Be Disturbed Again—14:10–11
   3.4. The Destruction of Israel's Enemies—14:12–15
4. Our Millennial Worship of the King over the Whole Earth Will Begin—14:16–21
   4.1. Jerusalem Will Be the Religious Center of the World—14:16

4.2. The Necessity of Worship—14:17–19
4.3. Israel's Central Role in the Worship of God—14:20–21

Exegetical Study

1. *Our Nations Will Fight Jerusalem for the Last Time—14:1–3*

A number of events lead up to this chapter, which records one of the darkest hours Israel will ever face in her history, or that the world has ever seen. In the first place, large numbers of Jewish people will be regathered back into the land, probably in unbelief. After a brief period of prosperity, the crisis mentioned in this chapter will overtake them as we enter into the last days. A treaty, or covenant, that had been made with Israel with the antichrist will have been broken after it had lasted for only three and a half years. In this covenant, Israel had sworn allegiance to a person other than the Messiah, but she was duped, as the antichrist here breaks his covenant and determines to commit genocide on the nation of Israel. The nations on planet earth will join antichrist as they march against Israel and Jerusalem. The attack on Jerusalem is graphically described in this chapter.

1.1. THE SIEGE OF JERUSALEM—14:1

This siege has already been presented in Zechariah 12:1–9, but it is presented there at a different stage in the event. Zechariah 14 presents the same siege, but at an earlier stage, before the Lord finally intervenes. In Zechariah 12:10–13:6, it speaks of the Lord's coming in grace and salvation, whereas in Zechariah 14, the Lord comes in power. The Lord's coming is for different purposes in each of the two chapters.

The time of the hostile siege against Israel is said to be in "a day of the Lord" (14:1), which is not a twenty-four hour day, but the period of time accompanied by the second coming of Messiah. This first verse of this chapter is the only place in Scripture where this last momentary triumph of the gentiles over Jerusalem is described.[1] Elsewhere in Scripture it deals more with the defeat of the gentile nations in this final battle at Jerusalem (Isa. 29:1–8; Joel 3; Zech. 12:1–9).

At this time, the spoil of Jerusalem will be divided among the nations. But it must be noticed that it is God himself who gathers the nations to come up to fight against Jerusalem (14:2); God will set the time and the site for this battle. So the end of the story is not yet in hand!

1.2. THE SUCCESS OF THE NATIONS—14:2

God often uses wicked hands to serve as his instruments of judgment. In a parallel chapter on Joel (chapter 8), we discussed in Joel 3:1–5 the four reasons why the nations of the world are summoned to this place. In Jeremiah 30:5–7, it is called "a time of trouble for Jacob."

The horrors of what will take place in that final battle against the city of Jerusalem are mind-boggling. They are as follows from Zechariah 14:2:

"the city will be captured,"

"the houses ransacked,"

"the women raped,"

"half the city will go into exile," and

"the rest of the people will not be taken from the city."

In the whole land of Israel, "two-thirds will be struck down" (13:8). Presumably, the remaining one-third will be brought through the fire of this event, refined as the people of God, a remnant.

1.3. A DELIVERER SHALL SAVE THE REMNANT—14:3

Just when the antichrist and the nations of the world will have seemed to have gained the upper hand, the Lord himself "will go out" (a military term) and "fight against those nations, as he fights in the day of battle" (14:3). It is for this reason that the Lord is also known as "a man of war" (Exod. 15:3, translation mine). When God enters a battle, you can be sure that the "battle is the LORD's" (1 Sam. 17:47). For just as God gave Gideon the victory on the day he fought for him and the few remaining in the army at Gibeon (Josh. 10:14), so will he demonstrate his power and win the victory in this final battle that is coming in Jerusalem.

2. Our Messiah Will Appear a Second Time on Earth—14:4–7

Where will he appear? Zechariah 14:4 says that "his feet will stand on the Mount of Olives" (the only reference in the Old Testament to the "Mount of Olives," even though 2 Sam. 15:30 has "the ascent of the Mount of Olives"). Two men dressed in white robes at the time of Jesus's ascension into heaven, after his resurrection, would later deliver this same teaching to his disciples in Acts 1:11: "This same Jesus, who has been taken from you into heaven, will come back in the same way as you have seen him go into heaven." Here, on the Mount of Olives, is where the glory of God had left Jerusalem earlier in Ezekiel 11:22–23. God had promised that that same glory would not return until he came back on the Mount of Olives and entered Jerusalem through the eastern gate (Ezek. 43:2). The Mount of Olives, of course, is the mile long projection of a limestone formation that stood about 200 feet above Zion, just to the east of the city of Jerusalem.

When will this happen? "On that day" (Zech. 14:4)—this timing device occurs seventeen times in Zechariah 12–14 alone. It is the same period of time that is connected with the events belonging to the second coming of Jesus.

What will take place at that time? As the Lord of Glory touches down on the Mount of Olives, it will split in two from east to west, thereby forming a valley down the middle of the Mount of Olives that will aid in the escape of those who have survived the attack on Jerusalem (14:4–5). In the book of Revelation (16:18–19), the seventh bowl is filled with the wrath of God in the form of an earthquake that will split Jerusalem into three parts as the nations simultaneously fall in defeat. As a result of the earthquake, a great plain will be formed from Geba to Rimmon (Zech. 14:10). In other words, the central highland region where Benjamin and Judah lived will be raised by seismic activity in that day. It will be as level as the Arabah. Geba is probably the same as Gibeah of Saul, about six miles north of Jerusalem, and Rimmon is about thirty-three miles southwest of Jerusalem, just north of Beersheba. Jerusalem's location remains the same, but it is transformed to accommodate its new status as the religious and governmental capital of the millennial earth. No wonder, for

> Great is the LORD, and most worthy of praise,
>   in the city of our God, his holy mountain.
> It is beautiful in its loftinesss,
>   the joy of the whole earth.
> Like the utmost heights of Zaphon is Mount Zion,
>   the city of the Great King. (Ps. 48:1–2)

Who will appear and with whom will he come? The Lord God will come in his great appearance (Zech. 14:5). He is the One who is the hope of Israel and the hope of the church. He will appear in his parousia along with his "holy ones" (5). These holy ones who accompany him are his angels, for the term "holy ones" is used of angels elsewhere (Deut. 33:3; Job 15:15; Ps. 89:5–7), yet the same term is also used for individuals (Lev. 11:44–45; 2 Chron. 35:3; Pss. 16:3; 34:9; Dan. 8:24). Likewise, the New Testament reveals that the Lord will be accompanied in his second advent with both his angels and his glorified saints (1 Thess. 3:13; Jude 14).

What will things be like after he, the Messiah, comes back to earth? The celestial luminaries will cease to function in their normal pattern. The sun and the moon will not give their light and the stars will withdraw their shining as well (Zech. 14:6–7; cf. Isa. 13:9–10; 24:23; Joel 3:14–16; Matt. 24:29–30; Mark 13:24–25; Rev. 6:13; 8:12). The resplendent light of the glory of the Lord will be reflected on earth, making the sun and the moon redundant. It will be a time when there will be neither cold nor frost (Zech. 14:6). When evening comes, it will still be light (7). It will be a day unlike any other in the history of the world! However, it is a day known completely by our Lord, so there is no need to worry about its timing or about any of its features and their impact on believers.

3. Our Messiah's Kingdom Will Be Established over All—14:8–15

3.1. It Will Issue Living Waters—14:8

In the restoration of Paradise lost, a life-giving stream will issue forth from the entrance of the sanctuary of God in Jerusalem. The psalmist talks about such a river "whose streams make glad the city of God" (Ps. 46:4). The prophet Joel likewise foretells a time when the brooks of Judah will flow full of water from the house of the Lord (Joel 3:18), and the prophet Ezekiel says it will water the entire desert of the Jordan (Ezek. 47:1–12). Zechariah points out that one-half of the water will flow to the eastern sea (= the Dead Sea), and the other half that flowed out of Jerusalem would flow to the western sea (= the Mediterranean Sea). There will be no stoppage of this flow either in summer or in winter (Zech. 14:8). This, in spite of the mounting scarcity of water currently in the Near Eastern countries, will take place!

3.2. The Lord Will Be Sovereign—14:9

In that day, the Lord himself will be King over the whole world (9). That is how Revelation 11:15 depicts the result of these events as well:

the world will be the kingdom of our Lord and of his Christ forever and ever from there on out (cf. Rev. 19:16).

Moreover, the Lord will be the only Lord, for he is the "one LORD" and "his name [is] the only name" (9). He is the incomparably great Lord, whose majesty and magnificence are without rival anywhere or at any time.

3.3. PEACE WILL NEVER BE DISTURBED AGAIN—14:10–11

That portion of the land, which previously was where Benjamin and Judah resided, will become level like the Arabah (10). Jerusalem itself will be physically uplifted as well! Moreover, Jerusalem's gates are listed here to show that that city will remain and will surely be inhabited once again (11). To the north, the "Benjamin Gate" is mentioned, which is probably the same as the gate of Ephraim, for that was the road that led north on through Benjamin to the tribe of Ephraim. The "First Gate," or "former gate," did not exist in Zechariah's time, but it was in the northeastern corner of Jerusalem. The "Corner Gate" was in the northwestern corner of the city. The "Tower of Hananel" seems to have stood in the north part of the city wall, while the "royal winepresses" were in the king's gardens on the south side of the city, thus giving to us the northern and southern borders of the city.

Three brief blessings are given in verse 11 on the city of Jerusalem. First, "it will be inhabited." She shall be forevermore at peace and no longer will they go out of Jerusalem in captivity, or in flight from the city. Second, "never again will it be destroyed[/cursed]." The word used for "destroyed" here is the Hebrew word *kherem*, meaning put under the "ban" by an involuntary curse. The old reasons for judging the nation, because of her sins, will be removed as a change comes in the lives of the people under the rule of God. Third, "Jerusalem will be secure." Even though it will no longer be surrounded by walls or fortifications, there will be no need to worry since the Lord himself will reside with his people in that city.

3.4. THE DESTRUCTION OF ISRAEL'S ENEMIES—14:12–15

Three weapons will be unleashed against Israel's enemies. The first is a deadly plague (12). The flesh of the enemy nations will "rot while they are standing on their feet." This will be a sudden and decisive plague. The eyes of the enemies will "rot in their sockets" and their tongues "will rot in their mouths." This seems to be similar to what happens from an atomic bomb blast.

Second, a "great panic" will overtake the attackers on the city of Jerusalem (13). The Lord will cause them to hear a roar, similar to what happened in the days of Gideon or in the days of Sennacherib's attempted invasion of Jerusalem. As they did in Gideon's day, the armies will turn on each other and destroy each other.

Third, the remnant of Judah will fight the enemy with what appears to be superhuman valor (14a). The booty Judah will collect will be enormous (14b).

4. Our Millennial Worship of the King over the Whole Earth Will Begin—14:16–21

4.1. JERUSALEM WILL BE THE RELIGIOUS CENTER OF THE WORLD—14:16

The survivors left from the attacking nations will go up to Jerusalem yearly to worship and adore the Lord of hosts (16). Another purpose for this annual trek to Jerusalem will be to celebrate the Feast of Tabernacles (16). This was the annual feast of ingathering (Lev. 23:33–44; Deut. 16:13–15). On the eighth day of the Feast of Tabernacles, all Israel returned to their own homes, a feature that looked forward to the homecoming of Israel and of the nations coming back to the Lord. As Revelation 21:3 announces, "Behold, the tabernacle of God is with men" (translation mine).

4.2. THE NECESSITY OF WORSHIP—14:17–19

The refusal of any nation to go up to worship God in Jerusalem year after year will result in a drought and the lack of rain for those people (18). Egypt is singled out, perhaps because they felt that since they historically got so little rainfall in a year anyway (less than an inch per year in Upper Egypt), and since the Nile River flowed so faithfully each year, they would be exempt from attending worship in Jerusalem. But God threatens Egypt and the other nations who similarly resist worshiping God that if they skip the Feast of Tabernacles (18–19) in Jerusalem, he will bring on them this plague of no rain.

4.3. ISRAEL'S CENTRAL ROLE IN THE WORSHIP OF GOD—14:20–21

Holiness to the Lord will be the "in" thing in that day. The "Canaanites" (21), who were the proverbial "merchants," will no longer trade or be present in the house of the Lord. On the contrary, everything will be dedicated to the Lord's use: the "bells on the horses," the "cooking pots in the LORD's house," and "every pot in Jerusalem and Judah" will be holy to the Lord (20). Israel will be cleansed in that day and so will all the nations who come to worship the Lord (cf. Zech. 3:1–10). The law of the house of the Lord will be holiness (Ezek. 43:12).

Conclusions

1. Psalm 72 promises that Jesus shall reign wherever the sun makes its journey. His kingdom will be spread out over the whole earth without any exceptions. The prophet Zechariah completes that same picture in chapter 14.
2. The nations of the earth will give one final try to destroy Jerusalem and to destroy the promise-plan God has offered in his history of salvation, but they will be broken in this final attempt to reject God and to overthrow his plan.
3. Christ will touch down on the Mount of Olives as he said he would and the earth will split open on the Mount of Olives forming a valley for those escaping the ravages of Jerusalem's attackers, while the land of Benjamin and Judah will be lifted up and become level like the Arabah, as the city of Jerusalem will also experience a topographical change.
4. In that day, the Lord will be the only King over the whole earth and his name the only name spoken of any longer by worshipers.

Part 6

The Coming Millennial Rule of Christ and the Arrival of the Eternal State

Few topics have created more controversy than the millennial question, with wonderful advocates on all three major sides: *pre*millennial, *a*millennial, and *post*millennial. Moreover, most think there is only one passage in the Scriptures that addesses this topic at all: Revelation 20:1–6, but that is what we hope to put to rest by showing that there are others to consider if we are to be faithful to the Word of God.

Nearly everybody will agree that the major millennial view of the early church in its first three or so centuries was a premillennial position. However, most people make the common assumption that in recent history premillennialism was held only by historic premillenarians or by dispensationalists. However, at the turn of the nineteenth into the twentieth century, four of the top five premillennialists were Reformed and Presbyterian in background. For example, Nathaniel West wrote his book *The Thousand Years*,[1] which exegetes a host of

Old Testament passages that demonstrate how relevant this position is for him and many of his fellow Reformed theologians.

One of the strongest passages Nathaniel West brought forward is the Isaiah 24:21–23 passage. It is astounding how similar some of the terms are in this Isaiah passage to John's terms in his Apocalypse. This study will return to that same passage once again.

But no survey of a group of texts on "last things" would be complete without introducing God's promise of a new heavens and a new earth. It is with this study that this collection of eschatological texts from the Old Testament will conclude.

Best of all is the promise in all of these events that Messiah will personally rule forever and ever. What is more, all of God's people who share his presence and fellowship will endure as long as he will, which also is forever and forever. Praise be to the King of kings and the Lord of lords!

14

The Millennial Rule and Reign of God

Isaiah 24:1–23

"In that day, the Lord will punish the powers . . . after many days."

Isaiah 24:21–22

Franz Delitzsch summarizes Isaiah 24–27 by saying,

> The cycle of prophecies which commences here has no other parallel in the Old Testament than perhaps Zech. [9–14]. Both sections are thoroughly eschatological and [apocalyptic] in their character, and start from apparently sharply defined historical circumstances, which vanish . . . for the simple reason, that the prophet lays hold of their radical idea, carries them out beyond their outward historical form, and uses them as emblems of far-off events of the last days.[1]

Accordingly, chapters 24–27 of Isaiah are closely linked to chapters 13–23 (Isaiah's prophecies against the nations), without a distinctive heading or title of their own. As such, Isaiah 24–27 completes the messages given to the nations as it depicts the coming end of

145

world history. Moreover, this relationship can be demonstrated by the prophet Jeremiah's use of Isaiah 24:17–18 in Jeremiah 48:43–44, as he reapplies the words Isaiah addressed to the whole world in general to the nation of Moab in particular. In that sense then, all the judgments made against each of the individual nations all flow into the last judgment that will come in the end day.

God's Millennial Rule

Text: Isaiah 24:1–23

Title: "God's Millennial Rule"

Focal Points: Verse 1, "See, the LORD is going to lay waste the earth and devastate it"; verses 21–22, "In that day, the LORD will punish the powers in the heavens above, and the kings on the earth below . . . [will] be punished after many days."

Homiletical Keyword: Features

Interrogative: What? (What are the features included in this laying waste to the earth and punishing the powers in the heavens above and the kings on earth below for "many days"?)

Teaching Aim: In the midst of the shaking of the foundations in the future, believers may rest confident that they can rely on the Lord to conclude all things well after the counsel of his will.

Outline

1. God Will Lay Waste the Whole World in a Future Day—24:1–13
    1.1. The Principle—24:1, 3a
    1.2. Those Included in This Event—24:2
    1.3. The Result of God's Judgment—24:3–6
    1.4. The Sadness It Brings—24:7–9
    1.5. Its Central City Is Removed—24:10–13
2. God Will Receive Universal Praise—24:14–16b
3. God Will Bring a Universal Upheaval on Earth—24:16c–20
4. God Will Then Rule as Triumphant King "After Many Days"—24:21–23

Exegetical Study

1. God Will Lay Waste the Whole World in a Future Day—24:1–13

As the rowdy songs of the unredeemed are silenced as we come to the end of the prophecies against the pagan nations, this new section of prophecies assures us that there is safety for all those who have trusted in the Lord. Therefore, the redeemed lift up their song all over the globe to the Lord God, who is the "Righteous One" (24:16), who will reign forever and ever.

1.1. THE PRINCIPLE—24:1, 3A

This chapter opens with a figure of speech known as an inclusio involving the terms "lay waste" in verse 1 and "laid waste" in verse 3. Moreover, it begins with "[For,] see[/behold], the LORD . . ."—a typical way for Isaiah to begin an important announcement, with "see/behold" accompanied by the divine name, followed by a participle, which in this case is the participle of "laying waste."[2] Thus, there can be little question that Isaiah is about to issue some startling news of a divine work that is to come. It will be a work that Yahweh alone is about to do.

The work anticipated here is that God is about to lay total waste to the natural and human worlds. Even though no justification has been given thus far for such drastic actions, nevertheless God will move in a final action against all. The picture will be completed, however, in verses 4–5 and in the remainder of the chapter, but most particularly in verses 18–20.

It is for these reasons that Isaiah 24–27 is called "the Little Book of Revelation," or "the Apocalypse of Isaiah." It centers on the "earth," for that term occurs some fifteen times in the opening chapter of this section. But the judgment of God extends even further, for even "the powers in the heavens" are struck with the same divine judgment (21–22), as the whole earth is made desolate and laid completely waste. Surely such devastation exceeds any previous judgment that God has worked in the history of civilization.

1.2. THOSE INCLUDED IN THIS EVENT—24:2

As the prophet moves on to describe the extent of this great judgment of God, six pairs of persons are listed. The six pairs are grouped as positions that are opposite one another:

priest versus people,

master versus servant,

mistress versus maid,

seller versus buyer,

borrower versus lender, and

debtor versus creditor.

What is striking about this sextet of pairs is that rank, wealth, or power are of no special significance in God's sight as it concerns his judgment. One group of persons will fare no better than the other when it comes to judgment, regardless of their position, wealth, status, or lack thereof. Only those who have put their trust in the Messiah, who is to come, will fare well. All other classes and strata of society will be seriously affected: "It will be the same" for all of them (2).

1.3. The Result of God's Judgment—24:3–6

As if to emphasize the certainty of the coming judgment at the conclusion of history, the Hebrew text repeats the two verbs ("lay waste" and "devastate/plunder") and adds two infinitive absolutes in verse 3 to emphasize the certainty and the reality of a major world shake-up. Such predictions are not from the fertile imagination or personal creation of the prophet Isaiah, but come from the inspiration of God, who now declares that the end of the world is anything but a natural end to the cosmic processes. True, other factors such as war, famine, and oppression may play a part in the permissive will of God, but in comparison to what God himself will do, these are minor motifs to say the most. God will bring a heap of destruction when he finishes with this old earth.

It is only because God has spoken that the prophet even dares to make such cataclysmic descriptions of a coming destruction. Thus, when God speaks, what can his messengers do except relay those same words to his people?

A reason for such devastation must be given, for it is mind-boggling in its range and in the effect of its destruction. And the reason is ready at hand: it is because of the sin that had accumulated on earth. That is why "the earth dries up and withers" (4a), for at that point the drought observed outwardly matches the internal blight that had reached the souls of mortals. One unusual expression, "the exalted of the earth" (4c), is unparalleled elsewhere in the Bible. But when mortals place themselves equal to or above the exalted God of the whole universe, there is trouble in store for this world of ours.

Verse 5 supplies us with three explanations for this stunning work of God:

1. "the earth is defiled by its people [who] have disobeyed [God's] laws,"
2. God's laws have been "violated," and
3. his "everlasting covenant" has been "broken," or nullified, by mortals.

In each case the charge is more serious. The word rendered "disobeyed" is the word for "transgressed." And the word for "laws" is the Hebrew word *torot* (the plural for the word *torah*), meaning not just the law of God, but also all his authoritative instructions. The plural form of this noun only appears eleven times in the Old Testament; therefore, it must either be a generalizing plural (whatever divine laws may have been violated), or a plural of application (laws covering every aspect of life). In the second charge, the word rendered "violated" is better translated as indicating that the people had "altered" or "replaced" what God in his law had said with what they had wanted that law to say. Even more devastating is the third case, where the word saying they had "broken" the covenant is a technical term, in which one sets aside the covenant and nullifies it. But neither our Lord, nor his Word, will take second seat or second place to anyone or anything else.

Notice that this indictment affects all the peoples of the earth. Yet some are hesitant to refer the "everlasting covenant" to the "Abrahamic-Davidic covenant," but attempt instead to refer it back to the Noahic covenant (Gen. 9:16). To be sure, God did call the covenant he made with Noah an "everlasting" covenant. Moreover, it is also true that this passage in Isaiah 24 does contain allusions to the flood of Noah. However, it is best to understand this "everlasting covenant" as the one that reached back to Abraham (Gen. 17:7, 13, 19; Ps. 105:9–10; cf. 1 Chron. 16:15–18), David (2 Sam. 23:5), and forward to a future Messiah (Isa. 55:3). The "law" God had given to David was a "law/charter for all humanity" (2 Sam. 7:19, translation mine), not one effective only for Israel. For just as the Abrahamic covenant was to be the means of blessing all the families of the earth (Gen. 12:3), so it is a universal offer here as well. The tripartite promise-plan formula declares, "I will be your God, you shall be my people, and I will dwell in the midst of you" (found almost fifty times throughout the Old and New Testaments). This promise-plan of God refers to all believers in all times of history.

Verse 6 twice stipulates a "therefore," implying God has come to a conclusion in this matter: "a curse consumes the earth" (6a). This curse is the very same one that had been predicted in Leviticus 26:25–45 and in Deuteronomy 11:26–28 and 28:15–68 of what would happen if God's people were to forget his Word and refuse to obey him. The people of the earth must now bear the guilt for the moral morass in which the earth is now staggering. That is why the earth's inhabitants must be punished by being "burned up" (6c). The Hebrew word *kharar* means "to be hot," despite the fact that it is ordinarily found in contexts where it means to be hot with anger, rather than to be consumed with fire. You may wonder, are any left after this judgment? The answer is yes, although "very few are left" (6c). These few are the evidence of the grace of God, the same grace that was seen in Noah's flood, where a remnant was preserved (Gen. 6:8; 7:7, 23; 8:16). However, the resulting depopulation will be described more fully in Isaiah 24:13.

1.4. The Sadness It Brings—24:7–9

It may be that the previous allusions to Noah are continued here as the references to the "new wine" and the "vine" (7) are used to depict the end of joy and merrymaking. What is clear is that no longer is the vine producing new wine. This too matches the drying up of the spiritual vitality of the people, which has now come upon the earth.

All the usual tokens of joy and celebration have ceased, including the "joyful harp" and the "gaiety of the tambourines" (8). There are no reasons left to celebrate anyway. Where joy in the Lord is failing, all other avenues of joy also give way to sadness and mourning.

1.5. Its Central City Is Removed—24:10–13

Unfortunately, this central city is not specifically identified, although there are a host of suggestions by commentators. Despite this fact, we read that this world-city of the Babylon-type is now quieted and devoid of all joyous festivals. "The entrance to every house is barred" (10) and the city now lies in ruins and finds itself left desolate. The houses are closed either because of the piles of rubble that bar the entrance to their doors, or because they have been shut to keep out any invaders.

The latter does not seem likely since the city is in ruins and remains "desolate" already.

Even the city's gates are "in ruins" (12), since they too must have previously been battered down in the contest for this city. But of even greater interest is the fact that what has happened to this city is what will be going on "among the nations" "on earth" (13). However, verse 13 makes the point that just as there are olives that are left on the tree after the olive tree has been beaten and there are gleanings left when the grape harvest has been taken, so God will leave a remnant of humanity. This is the imagery that Isaiah has already used for a remnant of Israel in 17:6. Therefore, a token group will be left from the whole group as the worldwide work of God's judgment proceeds.

2. God Will Receive Universal Praise—24:14–16b

The remnant just described in verse 13 is now the very same group who will "raise their voices" with a "shout for joy" as they come from the "west" and the "east" to "give glory to the LORD" and to "exalt the name of the LORD, the God of Israel" (14–15). It cannot be missed that the songs will originate from all over the world, i.e., from the "west," from the "east" (literally "lights," found only here in the Bible as a symbol for the "east"), and from the "islands," meaning the distant countries from the Mediterranean Sea and farther. Thus, singing and glorifying God will come from one end of the earth to the other. They will sing "Glory to the Righteous One" (16), for he is the Sovereign Lord who has triumphed indeed.

Such joyful song is in stark contrast to the devastation marked in the surrounding verses. But that is the contrast between the righteous and the unrighteous in that day. God will not abandon his own, but he will rise up in final judgment against all who have resisted him and refused to acknowledge him as their Lord and Savior.

3. God Will Bring a Universal Upheaval on Earth—24:16c–20

If what has been stated so far has seemed startling, what these verses reveal is even more earth-shaking—literally! By using an allusion to Noah's flood once again, the prophet under divine inspiration declares that God will open the "floodgates of heaven" (18), just as the foundations of the "deep" were opened in Noah's day (Gen. 7:11).

But now another image accompanies this one of a flood: an earthquake is described in verses 19–20. So powerful is this earthquake that the poor old earth just cannot take it. "The earth is broken up, . . . split asunder, [and] . . . thoroughly shaken" (19). Moreover, it "reels like a drunkard, it sways like a hut in the wind" (20), so violent is the seismic activity in that day. Already in Isaiah 1:8 the prophet has likened Jerusalem to a fragile "hut." The results of such an earthquake are enormous, to say the least.

Thus, while songs of praise are offered in verses 14–16, that praise is now followed by a new set of terrors stored up not only for unbelievers in Israel, but for those unbelievers in the whole world as well. Perhaps this is why verse 16c begins with "but I said." The prophet must have asked in effect: "But what about the events that still must come until the day God has his final triumph over sin and all evil on earth?" So stirred is the prophet that he feels he is being "made lean" (a much better rendering than the NIV's "waste away, waste away," 16c). The leanness Isaiah feels is one within his soul. That is why the prophet once again cries out, "Woe to me!" (16c, a refrain reminiscent of "Woe to me!" in 6:5). For now the prophet will use five Hebrew words, all derived from the same Hebrew root *bagad*, which point to plundering through deceit, or as we would say, deceit by pulling the wool over someone's eyes. But the effect of the eight English words that follow "Woe to me!" (these same five Hebrew words from the root *bagad*) sound like the tolling of a church bell in a funeral dirge. One act of God after another brings judgment upon judgment to the earth, as it is laid waste in that coming day of the Lord.

4. God Will Then Rule as Triumphant King "After Many Days"—24:21–23

This final section of this important prophecy begins with "in that day," which is the time when God will conclude the historic present time and prepare for the eternal state that is to come. Here in this final section, God will climax his work in history with an even greater work than what this old earth has seen so far. The judgments that are described in verses 1–20 on Israel and the haughty nations, as well as on the cosmic order, pale in significance to this climactic work of God.

God will judge not only "the powers in the heavens above," but he will also judge the terrestrial powers of "the kings of the earth below" (21). The aerial powers of the heavens probably include principalities, spiritual beings of darkness, and all sorts of wicked ones from the invisible realms of the evil one, which are headed up by Satan himself (Eph. 6:12), who is also called "the prince of the power of the air" and "the dragon and his angels" (Rev. 12:7–9; 20:1–3). Satan and his legions are depicted as being cast down from their lofty heights to be "herded together like prisoners bound in a dungeon" (Isa. 24:22). There in that "dungeon" they will be "shut up," or chained, so that they are restrained from any further assault on humanity or on this world, until their future release for a brief time followed by their final judgment at the end of the thousand-year rule of Messiah on this earth. This passage in Isaiah is parallel to Revelation 20:1–7 and Daniel 12:1.

In interpreting this passage, it is important to notice that the expression "after many days" (22; Hebrew *umerov yamim*) is the equivalent expression for the "thousand years" (Greek *chilia etē*) of Revelation 20:7, since the actions in both passages are identical and feature the imprisonment of Satan and his emissaries. Moreover, the judgments that precede both the "after many days" of Isaiah 24 and the "thousand years" of Revelation 20 are the same as those that follow that same period.

What God will do to Satan and his minions, he will do to the kings of the earth who are led by antichrist and his armies. This leader and his armies will be thoroughly vanquished at the second coming of our Lord. In this way, the visions of John in the book of Revelation are companion pieces to the prophecy of Isaiah. John does reveal later in Revelation 20:1–7 that as the one thousand years are coming to a close, Satan is released for a brief time from the abyss where he had been imprisoned, but finally he will be thrown into the lake of burning sulfur forever (Rev. 20:10).

So mind-boggling are these events of those final days of history on earth that the "moon" (literally, "the white one") and the "sun (literally, "the hot one") will be "ashamed" (Isa. 24:23), as if they were the ones responsible for the corruption of creation and the sin of its men and women. Joel 2:31 also speaks of the sun and the moon being darkened, but in their place a brighter light shines from heaven as the Lord of heaven and earth appears enthroned (Isa. 2:2–4; Obad. 21) in Zion (Jerusalem), and the final stage of the kingdom of God comes to earth as the millennial rule and reign of Christ begins (Rev. 21:2). Isaiah notes that Zion's elders, as representatives of all believers, rejoice as that reign of God begins on earth (Isa. 24:23; 60:1).

Conclusions

1. God brings the historic evil rule of the nations to a conclusion with a series of judgments on those nations.
2. God will hold one more judgment at the end of history against the devil and his angels for their part in sin and evil, and for the havoc they have created on earth.
3. Meanwhile, Satan and his hosts are locked up for "many days" (= the "thousand years"), while Christ rules on earth in a time of peace and security from Zion/Jerusalem.
4. The brilliance of the sun and the moon will look ashamed in the face of the majesty and brilliance of the Lord himself as he begins his reign in Jerusalem that will continue into the eternal state and last forever.

15

The New Creation

Isaiah 65:17–25; 66:18–24

"Behold, I will create new heavens and a new earth."

Isaiah 65:17

The key scriptural passages that speak of the new heavens and the new earth are Isaiah 65:17–25; 66:18–24; 2 Peter 3:13; and Revelation 21:1–4. The words used in the Hebrew and the Greek script for "new" refer not to a total discontinuity between the former universe and the cosmos that is to come. Instead the word "new" points to a "renewal" of the heavens and the earth; the Hebrew expression "the heavens and the earth" means the whole "universe," for Hebrew has no other term for the cosmos. In that sense, then, there are strong lines of continuity that in this case overcome the radical lines of discontinuity between the old heavens and earth and the "new." We will comment more on the word "new" later on.

The doctrine of the renewed universe is an important one, for it sets the record straight on what the life to come in eternity will be like. Some people dislike the Christian hymns that speak of the glories of that life to come in terms similar to those found in the hymn "My Jesus, I Love Thee."[1] Believers have sung for years, "In mansions of glory and endless delight, I'll ever adore Thee in heaven so bright."

But does this hymn exceed the teachings of the sacred page? Does not Jesus promise in John 14:1–3 that he will go ahead of us to heaven to prepare mansions for us? Therefore, "Let not your heart be troubled. . . . In my Father's house are many mansions; if it were not so, I would have told you. I go to prepare a place for you. And if I go and prepare a place for you, I will come again" (KJV).

True, heaven is not described in the Bible as some place far off in space, where God's men and women will be wearing white robes, strumming all day on harps, and singing for all they are worth as they flit from cloud to cloud. What is true is that we will be rejoined with our bodies, which we left behind at death; only they will now be improved bodies. So there is continuity with the old body just as Jesus's resurrected body still had the marks on his hands and feet from the nails on the cross and the mark on his side from the Roman spear driven there to see if he was still alive. But those bodies will also be accompanied with properties not seen before, demonstrated by the resurrected Jesus, who entered rooms where the doors were shut!

This doctrine of the renewed heaven and earth is also important because it completes the program of the redemptive plan of God. Ever since the fall of Adam and Eve, the creation has languished under the impact of the curse that came on it because of the sin of that first couple. But God will not leave it at that point, for he will usher in renewed heavens and a renewed earth, as Paradise is regained and restored back to what God had originally intended it to be at the creation.

Third, this doctrine is important because it is necessary to clearly demarcate the thousand years when Christ rules in the millennium from the final renewal of the heavens and the earth as we go into the eternal state. The Old Testament Scriptures repeatedly claim that the divine promise of the land to Israel will be fulfilled within history itself as a completion of the divine philosophy of history, for God will first finish in space and time what he promised in the Abrahamic covenant (Gen. 12:2–3). As with all the other divine promises (e.g., of a coming Seed and of the gospel), God will do in the historic process what he promised to do in regard to the "land" also. But this in no way short-circuits his commitment to a renewal of the heavens and the earth as believers move from history into the new era of eternity itself.

Some have argued, counter to Scripture, that Abraham understood the divine promise in Genesis 17:8 ("I will give as an everlasting possession [the whole land of Canaan] to you and to your descendants after you") in accordance with Hebrews 11:9–10 ("By faith [Abraham] made his home in the promised land like a stranger in a foreign country; he lived in tents, as did Isaac and Jacob, who were heirs with him of the same promise. For he was looking forward to the city with foundations, whose architect and builder is God"). Of course, all agree that the "city with foundations, whose architect and builder is God" can refer to none other than the city of Jerusalem. But the key question is this: is that city of Jerusalem to be found on the renewed earth as part of the eternal state, as amillennialists say, or is it to be found in the millennial rule and reign of Messiah prior to the eternal state, as premillennialists say? We will contend for the latter view as discussed in our chapter on Isaiah 2:2–5 (chapter 6). Scripture repeatedly states that the promise of this "everlasting possession" is not addressed to all the people of God, who in the widest sense are the "seed of Abraham," but is distinctively made first to Israel, as we have argued in our chapters on Zechariah 10:2–12 (chapter 5) and Ezekiel 37:1–28 (chapter 4).

However, when it is promised that there will be new heavens and a new earth, does that mean that the present universe will be annihilated so that a completely new universe will replace the present cosmos? Some interpreters favor such a complete discontinuity between the old and the new universe. However, that view of a complete disjuncture must be rejected for the following reasons.

The New Testament Greek word for newness is not the Greek word *neos*, but *kainos*. The former word designates something that is new in time or origin, but the latter word refers to something that is new in nature or quality. Therefore, what is taught in the new heavens and the new earth is not the emergence, or creation, of a brand new universe, but one that has continuity with the old, yet is thoroughly renewed. Moreover, there is an analogy between the newness referred to here, and the newness referred to in the resurrected bodies of believers. As we noted above, our resurrected bodies will have both a continuity and a discontinuity with our present bodies.

One New Testament text that might mislead some to think that this present universe will suffer a massive conflagration is 2 Peter 3:10: "But the day of the Lord will come like a thief. The heavens will disappear with a roar; the elements will be destroyed by fire and everything in it will be laid bare." Some manuscripts read for this final verb as if it said "will be burned up," but the better reading is found in most English texts as is rendered here in the NIV: "will be laid bare." Such a rendering also fits well with the understanding that the action being described in this verse is a renewal of the universe, and not a brand new replacement of the present cosmos.

The future, then, has both a break with the past as well as a connection with it; both continuity and discontinuity. The break is necessitated because of the forces of sin that must be broken by Christ and overcome by the power and might of his Word and his actions. But we must count on the power of the resurrection forces as being just as active and really present in this new work of God. Accordingly, the external "form" (Greek *schēma*) of this world is passing away (1 Cor. 7:31), but we can be sure that the same body of 1 Corinthians 15:44 that is put into the grave and decays is the same body that will be raised again to life with improvement.

The New Heavens and the New Earth in Eternity

Text: Isaiah 65:17–25; 66:18–24

Title: "The New Heavens and the New Earth in Eternity"

Focal Point: Isaiah 65:17, "Behold, I will create new heavens and a new earth. The former things will not be remembered, nor will they come to mind."

Homiletical Keyword: Distinctions

Interrogative: What? (What are the distinctions that will set the new heavens and new earth apart from the present universe?)

Teaching Aim: To show that this is a renewed universe that inaugurates the eternal state and is not to be confused with the reign of the Lord Jesus Christ during the millennium.

Outline

1. The Sound of Weeping and Crying Will Be No More—65:17–19
2. The Lives of Men and Women Will No Longer Be Cut Short—65:20–24
3. The Lives of Animals Will Be Changed—65:25
4. The Heavens and the Earth Will Endure Forever—66:18–24

Exegetical Study

1. *The Sound of Weeping and Crying Will Be No More—65:17–19*

As a substantiation for all that has gone on from Isaiah 56:1 ("Maintain justice and do what is right, for my salvation is close at hand and my righteousness will soon be revealed") through Isaiah 65:17, this verse begins with "for behold." The NIV has suppressed the translation of the word "for," but this text is intended to answer the question, why "maintain justice and do what is right"? Therefore, in order to answer this question, this passage will show how mortals are able to live out the righteousness of God. There is only one way to do that: if God intervenes and remakes us and our world as it was before the fall of Adam and Eve, then it will be possible. God must do all over again what he did the first time in his original creation.

God is able to remake this world as he created it the first time. Accordingly, humans should maintain justice and practice righteousness in anticipation of the time when the power of God will be manifested once again as he renews the heavens and the earth. Just as the language of Isaiah 40–48 uses similar ideas when it promises that God will do a "new thing" by delivering Israel from Babylon, so God will bring a "new thing" into being by bringing forth new heavens and a new earth and by dealing with sin, which has had dominion over the earth and the heavens since the fall.

This promise of God to renew the universe is "in keeping with his [old] promise" (2 Pet. 3:13). The former universe will "disappear with a roar" as it is destroyed by fire, thereby laying everything in it bare (2 Pet. 3:10). "The former things will not be remembered, nor will they come to mind" (65:17), God announces to the prophet Isaiah. In its place, God will "create Jerusalem to be a delight and its people a joy" (18). No longer will weeping and crying be heard anymore (19), for God will wipe away both the effects and the memory of sin (Rev. 21:4).

Such news is unprecedented, for all too long now sin has left in its trail shame and sorrow. This will all be exchanged for a joy and a delight, because of what God will create in his renewal of the heavens and the earth. So significant is this note of rejoicing and gladness that it is repeated three times in verses 18–19!

God will adopt Jerusalem for himself. That is why Revelation 21:2 depicts a new Jerusalem coming down out of heaven. It will be from this city that the teaching of the Lord Jesus himself will go forth as the nations of the world will gather annually in Jerusalem to be instructed and to worship the Lord (Isa. 2:2–4). The fact that the new Jerusalem comes down from heaven indicates that God will be the source of this renewed city.

Some biblical texts call for the perpetuity of the earth, as for example Psalm 104:5, which reads, "He set the earth on its foundations;

it can never be moved." Again, in Psalm 148:6, it also teaches, "He set [the sun, moon, stars, and the heavens] in place for ever and ever; he gave a decree that will never pass away." It is for such reasons in these and other similar texts that the better reading in 2 Peter 3:10 is that the heavens and the earth "will be laid bare," not that they "will be burned up" and thus destroyed.

2. The Lives of Men and Women Will No Longer Be Cut Short—65:20–24

These verses are generally regarded as some of the most difficult to interpret. They should not be read as a contradiction to Isaiah 25:6–9 and 26:18–19, for the general sense is clear, even if the precise nuances of each word may not be certain. The point of Isaiah 65:20–24 is that in the future one may disregard any thoughts of an untimely death.

One way to overcome the difficult verses is to interpret the "Jerusalem" of verses 17–19 altogether differently from the "Jerusalem" of verses 20–24. If this interpretation (an unusual one to be sure) is true, then this later Jerusalem is the Jerusalem of the millennial kingdom, which occurs one thousand years before the new heavens and new earth appear. The reason I take this view is because when the universe is renewed in eternity, sin, sorrow, and death will no longer appear, while all of them still appear in the millennial kingdom. Death, sin, and sorrow do appear in the millennial kingdom, for Satan is released for a short period of time at the end of the thousand years before he is once and for all cast into the lake of fire to abide there forever. Yet during the millennium, death is so rare that it can be said, "Never again will there be in [Jerusalem] an infant who lives but a few days" (20a–b). Moreover, "an old man who does not live out his years; [or] . . . who dies a hundred will be thought a mere youth; [or] he who fails to reach a hundred will be considered accursed" (20c–g). This seems to indicate that Isaiah is teaching that death during this time will be extremely rare. Even the presence of one who might be "accursed" raises the question as to whether that one has not been cursed for a good reason.

But none of this will be happening during the time of the renewal of the universe in the eternal state. On the other hand, one wonders why God would allow even this small amount of evil to be present when he, the Lord, is present. One reason may be that with the devil out of the way and in prison for most of the thousand years, it will show what a lame excuse some have given for their sinning in the present era. The excuse, "I sinned because the devil made me do it" will certainly not apply in that day. Instead, so strong will the call for obedience to divine things be evidenced that the old excuses will plainly be passé.

The joy of life will consist of building houses and living in them, planting vineyards and eating the fruit that comes from them (21–22). This is what had been promised under the laws of Moses in Deuteronomy 28:1–14.

So enduring and secure will the people of God be in those days that they will last "as the days of a tree" (22). The staples of life will be long life and joyful appreciation for all it has to offer.

Even more promising is the fact that no labor or toil will be regarded as "in vain" (23). With all frustration and futility removed from the earth, all of living will at once be a joy and a source of great satisfaction. Children born during the millennium (if we are right in regarding this section as speaking of that thousand-year period of time, instead of the eternal state) will not be "doomed to misfortune," for they too will be blessed by the Lord (23).

One more gift is added from God: God will answer our prayers before we call upon him, or even while we are still speaking (24). No longer will sin block access to our Lord, for he will promptly respond to all our requests that are made to him.

3. The Lives of Animals Will Be Changed—65:25

Isaiah has already raised this topic in 11:6–9. In the messianic age, the effects of God's new creation work will be seen in the way that the carnivorous animals, such as the lion and the wolf, will no longer bother such domesticated animals as lambs (25a). All of these animals will now be able to feed together. What is more, the lion will also need to have some type of gastronomical change, for it too will eat straw just like an ox (25b).

The surprising part of this text is that "dust will be the serpent's food" (25c). Does this text allude to Genesis 3:14, where in the garden of Eden the serpent was cursed and wrecked by sin so that his defeat was put in terms of being fed with dirt, just as we say in an athletic contest, "Let the opponents bite the dust"? There is no doubt that "the serpent" was condemned to crawl on his belly and bite the dust, as we say, in defeat.

4. The Heavens and the Earth Will Endure Forever—66:18–24

Once again, the prophet reverts back to the topic of Isaiah 65:17–25, where he speaks of "new heavens and a new earth." Even though Israel will suffer a Diaspora among the nations of the world (66:18–19), God will gather all the nations to see what he will do for them by his divine glory (18). But God will bring both Israel and "[their] brothers" forth "from all the nations, to [his] holy mountain in Jerusalem" (20). Even more astounding is the fact that God will select some of these gentile nations to be "priests and Levites" (21). This must have shocked some of Israel's theological instincts for sure!

"All mankind" (23) will come up to Jerusalem month after month and Sabbath after Sabbath (Zech. 14:16–21) to worship the Lord. The redeemed of the Lord will encompass men and women from every race, tribe, and language!

God will also make the renewed heavens and earth "endure" before him just as he will make the name of those who believe and their descendants "endure" (22). Therefore the destiny of the remnant of Israel who believed will be the grounds not only for their sure return to the land of Israel; it will also be the grounds for the blessings that will come to the gentiles as well.

This passage ends with the horrific destiny of the ungodly. The godly "will go out and look upon the dead bodies of those who rebelled against [God]" (24). This may seem to be somewhat crude and offensive, but recall how long the redeemed have had to watch goodness, justice, truth, and righteousness be handed defeat after defeat in their lifetimes. This examining of what God has done is not for the purpose of gloating over the destruction of the wicked, but it is to see that both sides of the promise-plan of God are true. God's threats are just as true and secure as are his promises of blessing.

The picture of the final end of the wicked is the basis for the most frequently cited description of hell given by Jesus during his time on this earth as recorded in the Gospels. The imagery comes from the "Valley of Hinnom," later known as Ge-Hinnom or Gehenna. This is the site just outside of Jerusalem where the Israelites offered their firstborn to gods such as Molech to be burned alive as sacrifices. However, so despicable was this practice, as it was later realized, that this same spot became the city dump, a place where "the worm [did] not die [as it fed on the garbage in the dump]; nor [was the] fire quenched [as the wind frequently stirred up the smoldering embers back into full flame]" (24). Thus the God-rejecting group will be subject to everlasting torment throughout all eternity.

Conclusions

1. As history concludes with the thousand-year rule and reign of Christ on this earth (= millennium), eternity will commence as God recreates the heavens and earth.
2. Even though evil may raise its ugly head briefly during the millennium, so rare will be death, sorrow, and sin that a person who dies at age one hundred will seem like a young child dying.
3. In the eternal state, people will be able to enjoy the homes they have built along with the fruit of the vineyards they have planted.
4. The renewed heavens and the renewed earth will not fade away, but they will endure forever, along with Israel and all the gentiles who have believed on the name of the Lord.

Selected Bibliography

Allis, O. T. *Prophecy and the Church*. Philadelphia: P&R, 1945.

Anderson, Robert. *The Coming Prince*. London: Hodder & Stoughton, 1894.

Andrews, Richard J. "The Political and Religious Groups Involved with Building the Third Temple." MA thesis, Indiana University, 1995.

Ariel, Rabbi Yisrael. *The Odyssey of the Third Temple*. Translated and adapted by Chaim Richman. Jerusalem: G. Israel Publications and Productions, Ltd. and the Temple Institute, 1994.

Armes, Paul. "The Concept of Dying in the Old Testament." PhD diss., Southwestern Baptist Theological Seminary, 1981.

Bailey, Lloyd R. *Biblical Perspectives on Death*. Philadelphia: Fortress, 1979.

Beecher, Willis J. *The Prophets and the Promise*. Grand Rapids: Baker, 1963. First published 1905 by Thomas Y. Crowell.

Berkhof, Hendrikus. *Christ the Meaning of History*. Richmond: John Knox, 1966.

Bertholet, Alfred. "Eschatology in the History of Religion." In *Twentieth Century Theology in the Making*. Edited by Jaarslav Pelikan. New York: Harper, 1969.

Blackstone, William E. *Jesus Is Coming*. London: Fleming H. Revell, 1908.

Block, Daniel I. "Beyond the Grave: Ezekiel's Vision of Death and Afterlife." *Bulletin for Biblical Research* 2 (1992): 113–41.

Bloomfield, Arthur. *Where Is the Ark of the Covenant and What Is Its Role in Biblical Prophecy?* Minneapolis: Dimension Books, 1976.

Boettner, Loraine. *The Millennium*. Grand Rapids: Baker, 1958.

Bonar, Horatius. *Prophetical Landmarks*. London: James Nisbet, 1876.

Boutflower, Charles. *In and around the Book of Daniel*. 1928; repr., Grand Rapids: Kregel, 1977.

Bright, John. *Covenant and Promise: The Prophetic Understanding of the Future in Pre-Exilic Israel*. Philadelphia: Westminster, 1976.
———. *The Kingdom of God*. Nashville: Abingdon-Cokesbury, 1953.
Brueggemann, Walter. *The Land: Place as Gift, Promise, and Challenge in Biblical Faith*. 2nd ed. Minneapolis: Fortress, 2002.
Clouse, Robert G., ed. *The Meaning of the Millennium*. Downers Grove, IL: InterVarsity, 1977.
Corley, B. "The Jews, the Future, and God (Romans 9–11)." *Southwestern Journal of Theology* 19, no. 1 (1976): 42–56.
Culver, Robert D. *Daniel and the Latter Days: A Study in Millennialism*. Rev. ed. Chicago: Moody, 1977.
Davies, P. R. "Eschatology in the Book of Daniel," *Journal of Theological Studies* 17 (1980): 33–53.
Davies, W. D. *The Gospel and the Land*. Berkeley: University of California Press, 1974.
Doukhan, Jacques B. *Israel and the Church: Two Voices for the Same God*. Peabody, MA: Hendrickson, 2002.
Dumbrell, William J. *The Search for Order: Biblical Eschatology in Focus*. Grand Rapids: Baker, 1994.
Goldsworthy, Graeme. *Gospel and Kingdom: A Christian Interpretation of the Old Testament*. Carlisle, UK: Paternoster, 1994.
Gowan, Donald E. *Eschatology in the Old Testament*. Philadelphia: Fortress, 1986.
Gruber, Daniel. *The Church and the Jews: The Biblical Relationship*. Springfield, MO: General Council of the Assemblies of God, 1991.
Gunkel, Hermann. *Schöpfung und Chaos im Urzeit und Endzeit*. 1895. Translated by K. William Whitney Jr. Reprinted as *Creation and Chaos in the Primeval Era and the Eschaton: A Religio-Historical Study of Genesis 1 and Revelation 12*. Grand Rapids: Eerdmans, 2006.
Hasel, Gerhard F. "The Identification of 'The Saints of the Most High' in Daniel 7." *Biblica* 56 (1975): 173–92.
Hoekema, Anthony A. *The Bible and the Future*. Grand Rapids: Eerdmans, 1979.
Hoffman, Yair. "Eschatology in the Book of Jeremiah." In *Eschatology in the Bible and in Jewish and Christian Tradition*, 75–97. Sheffield: Sheffield Academic Press, 1997.
Holwerda, David E. *Jesus and Israel: One Covenant or Two?* Grand Rapids: Eerdmans, 1995.
Horner, Barry E. *Future Israel: Why Christian Anti-Judaism Must Be Challenged*. Nashville: Broadman & Holman, 2007.
Hubbard, David A. "Hope in the Old Testament." *Tyndale Bulletin* 34 (1983): 34–53.
Huey, F. B. "The Hebrew Concept of Life after Death in the Old Testament," ThD diss., Southwestern Baptist Theological Seminary, 1962.

Ice, Thomas, and Ransall Price. *Ready to Rebuild*. Eugene, OR: Harvest House, 1992.

Jeffrey, Grant R. *Armageddon: Appointment with Destiny*. New York: Bantam Books, 1990.

Jenni, E. "Das Wort '*ôlām* im Alten Testament." *Zeitschrift für die alttestamentliche Wissenschaft* 64 (1952): 197–248.

Johnston, Philip S. *Shades of Sheol: Death and Afterlife in the Old Testament*. Downers Grove, IL: InterVarsity, 2002.

Juster, Dan, and Keith Intrater. *Israel, the Church, and the Last Days*. Shippensburg, PA: Destiny Image Publishers, 1990.

Kaiser, Otto. *Death and Life*. Translated by John Steely. Nashville: Parthenon, 1981.

Kaiser, Walter C., Jr. "An Assessment of 'Replacement Theology.'" *Mishkan* 21 (February 1994): 9–20.

———. "Ezekiel 37 and the Promise-Plan of God: The Divine Restoration of Israel." In *Jews and the Gospel at the End of History: A Tribute to Moishe Rosen*, 185–99. Grand Rapids: Kregel, 2009.

———. "Israel and Its Land in Biblical Perspective." In *The Old Testament in the Life of God's People: Essays in Honor of Elmer A. Martens*, edited by Jon Isaak, 245–56. Winona Lake, IN: Eisenbrauns, 2009.

———. "Israel as the People of God." In *The People of God: Essays on the Believers' Church*, edited by Paul Basden and David S. Dockery, 99–108. Nashville: Broadman, 1991.

———. "Psalm 72: An Historical and Messianic Current Example of Antiochene Hermeneutical *Theoria*," *Journal of the Evangelical Theological Society* 52, no. 2 (June 2009): 257–70.

———. "The Land of Israel and the Future Return (Zechariah 10:6–12)." In *Israel, the Land and the People: An Evangelical Affirmation of God's Promises*, edited by H. Wayne House, 168–85. Grand Rapids: Kregel, 1998.

———. *The Promise-Plan of God: A Biblical Theology of the Old and New Testaments*. Grand Rapids: Zondervan, 2008.

Kellogg, Samuel H. *The Jews; or Prediction and Fulfillment; An Argument for the Times*. New York: Anson D. F. Randolf & Co., 1883.

Knibb, Michael A. "Life and Death in the Old Testament." In *The World of Ancient Israel*, edited by R. E. Clements, 395–415. Cambridge: Cambridge University Press, 1989.

Koenen, Klaus. "Eschatology in the Old Testament." *Zeitschrift für die alttestamentliche Wissenschaft* 113 (2001): 136–37.

Ladd, George E. *Crucial Questions about the Kingdom of God*. Grand Rapids: Eerdmans, 1952.

———. *The Gospel of the Kingdom: Scriptural Studies in the Kingdom of God*. Grand Rapids: Eerdmans, 1959.

LaRondelle, Hans K. *The Israel of God in Prophecy: Principles of Prophetic Interpretation*. Berrien Springs, MI: Andrews University Press, 1983.

LaSor, William S. *The Truth About Armageddon*. San Francisco: Harper & Row, 1982.

Lindsay, Hal. *The Late Great Planet Earth*. Grand Rapids: Zondervan, 1970.

Ludwigson, Ray. *A Survey of Bible Prophecy*. Grand Rapids: Zondervan, 1951.

MacPherson, Dave. *The Unbelievable Pre-Trib Origin*. Kansas City: Heart of American Bible Society, 1973.

Mayhue, Richard L., and Robert L. Thomas. *The Master's Perspective of Biblical Prophecy*. Grand Rapids: Kregel, 2002.

McClain, Alva J. *Daniel's Prophecy of the Seventy Weeks*. Grand Rapids: Zondervan, 1940.

McCullough, W. S. "Israel's Eschatology from Amos to Daniel." In *Studies on the Ancient Palestinian World*, edited by F. S. Winnet and D. B. Redford, 86–101. Toronto Semitic Texts and Studies 2. Toronto: University of Toronto Press, 1972.

Murphy, Roland E. "History, Eschatology and the Old Testament." *Continuum* 7 (1970): 583–93.

Nassif, Bradley. "Antiochene *Theoria* in John Chrysostom's Exegesis, PhD diss., Fordham University, 1991.

Payne, J. Barton. *Encyclopedia of Biblical Prophecy*. New York: Harper & Row, 1973.

Pentecost, J. Dwight. *Things to Come*. Findlay, OH: Dunham Publishing Co, 1958.

Peters, George N. H. *The Theocratic Kingdom*. 1884; repr., Grand Rapids: Kregel, 1988.

Price, Randall. *In Search of Temple Treasures*. Eugene, OR: Harvest House, 1994.

Price, Walter K. *The Prophet Joel and the Day of the Lord*. Chicago: Moody, 1976.

Reventlow, Henning Graf. *Eschatology in the Bible and in Jewish and Christian Tradition*. Sheffield: Sheffield Academic Press, 1997.

Robertson, O. Palmer. *The Israel of God: Yesterday, Today, and Tomorrow*. Phillipsburg, NJ: P&R, 2000.

Rosenberg, Joel C. *Epicenter*. Carol Stream, IL: Tyndale, 2006.

Routledge, Robin. "God and the Future." In *Old Testament Theology: A Thematic Approach*, 261–310. Downers Grove, IL: IVP Academic, 2008.

———. "God and the Nations." In *Old Testament Theology: A Thematic Approach*, 311–34. Downers Grove, IL: IVP Academic, 2008.

Russell, D. S. *Apocalyptic Ancient and Modern*. London: SCM, 1978.

Satterthwaite, Philip E., Richard S. Hess, and Gordon J. Wenham. *The Lord's Anointed: Interpretation of Old Messianic Texts*. Tyndale House Studies. Carlisle: Paternoster; Grand Rapids: Baker, 1995.

Sauer, Erich. *From Eternity to Eternity*. Grand Rapids: Eerdmans, 1954.

Sawyer, J. F. A. "Hebrew Words for Resurrection." *Vetus Testamentum* 23 (1973): 218–34.

Schmitt, John W., and J. Carl Laney. *Messiah's Coming Temple: Ezekiel's Prophetic Vision of the Future Temple*. Grand Rapids: Kregel, 1997.

Shedd, William G. T. *The Doctrine of Endless Punishment*. New York: Scribner, 1886.

Smith, Wilbur M. *Israeli/Arab Conflict and the Bible*. Glendale, CA: Regal, 1967.

Stacey, W. D. "Man as Soul." *Expository Times* 72 (1961): 349–50.

Tasker, R. V. G. "Wrath." In *The New Bible Dictionary*. London: Inter-Varsity Fellowship, 1962.

Van der Ploeg, J. P. M. "Eschatology in the Old Testament." In *The Witness of Tradition*, 89–99. *Oudtestamentlische Studiën* 17. Leiden: Brill, 1972.

Vawter, Bruce. "Intimations of Immortality and the Old Testament." *Journal of Biblical Literature* 91 (1972): 158–71.

Vriezen, T. C. "Prophecy and Eschatology." In *Congress Volume, Copenhagen*, 199–229. Supplements to *Vetus Testamentum* 1. Leiden: Brill, 1953.

Walvoord, John F. *Daniel, the Key to Prophetic Revelations: A Commentary*. Chicago: Moody, 1971.

Wright, Christopher. "A Christian Approach to Old Testament Prophecy Concerning Israel." In *Jerusalem Past and Present in the Purpose of God*, edited by P. W. L. Walker, 1–19. Cambridge: Tyndale, 1992.

Zimmerli, Walther. *Man and His Hope in the Old Testament*. London: SCM, 1971.

Notes

Introduction

1. As noted by Ralph L. Smith in *Old Testament Theology: Its History, Method, and Message* (Nashville: Broadman & Holman, 1993), 373.

2. *Dictionary of the Bible*, ed. James Hastings (New York: Charles Scribner's Sons, 1909), s.v. "eschatology" by Shaler Matthews, Internet Archive online, http://www.archive.org/stream/cu31924029271223#page/n256/mode/1up/search/eschatology.

3. J. P. M. Van der Ploeg, "Eschatology in the Old Testament," in *The Witness of Tradition*, Oudtestamentlische Studiën 17, ed. A. S. Woude (Leiden: Brill, 1972), 89.

4. Sigmund Mowinckel, *He That Cometh*, trans. G. W. Anderson (1956; repr., Grand Rapids: Eerdmans, 2005), 125.

5. John Bright, *Covenant and Promise: The Prophetic Understanding of the Future in Pre-Exilic Israel* (Philadelphia: Westminster, 1976), 21–22.

6. See Willis J. Beecher, *The Prophets and the Promise* (1905; repr., Grand Rapids: Baker, 1970), 310–11; also Walter C. Kaiser Jr., *The Promise-Plan of God: A Biblical Theology of the Old and New Testaments* (Grand Rapids: Zondervan, 2008), 161.

7. For further discussion of these terms, see Oscar Cullmann, "The Significance of the New Testament Terminology for Time," in *Dimensions of Faith*, ed. William Kimmel and Geoffrey Cline (New York: Twayne, 1960), 305–40, and Joachim Guhrt, "Time," in *The New International Dictionary of New Testament Theology*, ed. Colin Brown (Grand Rapids: Zondervan, 1978), 3:826–33.

8. Darrell L. Bock. "The Reign of the Lord Jesus," in *Dispensationalism, Israel, and the Church*, ed. Craig Blaising and Darrell L. Bock (Grand Rapids: Zondervan, 1992), 46; emphasis mine.

9. See the definitive work by E. W. Bullinger, *Figures of Speech Used in the Bible* (1898; repr., Grand Rapids: Baker, 2003).

Chapter 1 Life and Death in the Old Testament

1. See R. Laird Harris, "The Meaning of the Word Sheol as Shown by Parallels in Poetic Texts," *Journal of the Evangelical Theological Society* 4 (1961): 129–35.

2. T. D. Alexander, "The Psalms and the Afterlife," *Irish Biblical Studies* 9 (1987): 2–17.

Chapter 2 The Resurrection of Mortals in the Old Testament

1. Mitchell Dahood, *Psalms 1 (1–50)*, Anchor Bible (New York: Anchor, 1965), xxxvi.
2. Mitchell Dahood, *Psalms 3 (101–150)*, Anchor Bible (New York: Doubleday, 1970), xlv–lii.
3. Bruce Vawter, "Intimations of Immortality in the Old Testament," *Journal of Biblical Literature* 91 (1972): 158–71.
4. J. F. A. Sawyer, "Hebrew Words for Resurrection," *Vetus Testamentum* 23 (1973): 220.
5. This list was supplied by Ralph L. Smith, *Old Testament Theology: Its History, Method, and Message* (Nashville: Broadman & Holman, 1993), 393.
6. William Henry Green, *The Argument of the Book of Job Unfolded* (1874; repr., Minneapolis: James & Klock, 1977), 191.
7. Ibid., 216–17 (emphasis mine).

Chapter 4 The Future Resurrection and Reunification of the Nation

1. Daniel I. Block, *The Book of Ezekiel: Chapters 25–48*, New International Commentary on the Old Testament, vol. 2 (Grand Rapids: Eerdmans, 1998), 379.
2. Peter C. Craigie, *Ezekiel*, Daily Study Bible (Louisville: Westminster John Knox, 1983), 261.

Chapter 6 The Branch of the Lord and the New Zion

1. Donald E. Gowan, *Eschatology in the Old Testament* (Philadelphia: Fortress, 1986), 3. Original reads: "Jerusalem appears with a prominence unparalleled by any other theme. It was surprising to find a 'center' of OT eschatology."
2. Ibid., 4–6.
3. Ibid., 8nn11–17.

Chapter 7 The Extent of Messiah's Rule and Reign

1. J. Barton Payne, *Encyclopedia of Biblical Prophecy* (New York: Harper & Row, 1973), 257.
2. H. C. Leupold, *Exposition of Psalms* (Grand Rapids: Baker, 1974), 21–23.
3. Walter C. Kaiser Jr., *The Messiah in the Old Testament* (Grand Rapids: Zondervan, 1995), 92–135.
4. James E. Smith, *What the Bible Teaches about the Promised Messiah* (Nashville: Thomas Nelson, 1993), 90–209.
5. Much of the material that follows is an expansion of my article "Psalm 72: An Historical and Messianic Current Example of Antiochene Hermeneutical *Theoria*," *Journal of the Evangelical Theological Society* 52, no. 2 (June 2009): 257–70.
6. Bradley Nassif, "Antiochene *Theoria* in John Chrysostom's Exegesis" (PhD diss., Fordham University, 1991).
7. Ibid., 55. Nassif cites from the Latin in A. Vaccari, "La '*Theoria*' Nella Scula Esegetica di Antiochia," *Biblica* 1 (1920): 20–22. The English translation is one Nassif commissioned.
8. Willis J. Beecher, *The Prophets and the Promise* (1905; repr., Grand Rapids: Baker, 1970), 130.
9. Walter Brueggemann and Patrick D. Miller, "Psalm 73 as Canonical Marker," *Journal for the Study of the Old Testament* 72 (1996): 45–56.

10. G. H. Wilson, "The Use of Royal Psalms at the 'Seams' of the Hebrew Psalter," *Journal for the Study of the Old Testament* 35 (1986): 85–94.

11. Christopher Seitz, "Royal Promises in the Canonical Books of Isaiah and Psalms," in *Isaiah in Scripture and the Church* (unpublished manuscript, 1994), cited in Brueggemann and Miller, "Psalm 73 as Canonical Marker," 51n17.

12. Smith, *What the Bible Teaches*, 195.

13. Charles A. Briggs, *Messianic Prophecy* (New York: Charles Scribner's Sons, 1889), 137–40.

14. So comments Mitchell Dahood, *Psalms II: 51–100*, Anchor Bible (New York: Doubleday, 1968), 179.

15. For further elaboration on this point, see Walter C. Kaiser Jr., "The Blessing of David: The Charter for Humanity," in *The Law and the Prophets: Old Testament Studies in Honor of Oswald Thompson Allis*, ed. John H. Skilton (Phillipsburg, NJ: P&R, 1974), 298–318.

16. A. A. Anderson, *The Book of Psalms*, New Century Bible Commentary (Grand Rapids: Eerdmans, 1972), 2:525.

17. O. T. Allis, "The Blessing of Abraham," *Princeton Theological Review* 25 (1927): 263–98. See also Kaiser, *Promise-Plan of God*, esp. 17–67.

18. Isaac Watts, "Jesus Shall Reign Where'er the Sun" (1791), in *The Psalms and Hymns of Isaac Watts* (1806), no. 156, vv. 1, 5, http://www.hymnary.org/text/jesus_shall _reign_whereer_the_sun.

19. James Montgomery, "Hail to the Lord's Anointed" (1821), in *Sacred Poems and Hymns* (1854), no. 267, v. 1, http://www.hymnary.org/text/hail_to_the_lords_anointed.

Chapter 8 The Arrival of the Day of the Lord

1. Scholars have assigned Joel and Obadiah to every date from the ninth century to the sixth century BC, but a good case can be made for the ninth century. See Walter C. Kaiser Jr., *A History of Israel: From the Bronze Age through the Jewish Wars* (Nashville: Broadman & Holman, 1998), 336–37.

Chapter 9 Gog and Magog

1. Joel C. Rosenberg, *Epicenter* (Carol Stream, IL: Tyndale, 2006), esp. 159–70.

2. I am especially indebted to Joel Rosenberg for help in interpreting this list of nations (*Epicenter*, 128–32).

Chapter 10 The Seventy Weeks of Daniel

1. J. A. Montgomery, *A Critical and Exegetical Commentary on the Book of Daniel*, International Critical Commentary (Edinburgh: T&T Clark, 1927), 400–401.

2. Jacques Doukhan, "The Seventy Weeks of Daniel 9: An Exegetical Study," *Andrews University Seminary Studies* 17 (1978): 1 (emphasis in the original).

3. In calculating time from BC to AD, one year must be omitted, for there is no 0 BC. Then one must add, warned Sir Robert Anderson, 116 leap days (173,740 + 116) with another twenty-four days from March 14, 32 AD, until April 6, 32 AD, to work back from our Julian calendar.

4. Harold W. Hoehner, *Chronological Aspects of the Life of Christ* (Grand Rapids: Zondervan, 1977).

5. See for further critique Allen A. MacRae, *The Prophecies of Daniel* (Singapore: Christian Life Publishers, 1991), 193–202.

6. See Kaiser, *History of Israel*, 469–75.

Chapter 11 The New Coming Third Temple in Jerusalem

1. See Rabbi Levi Brackman and Rivkah Lubitch, "Survey: 64 Percent Want Temple Built," *Jewish World*, July 30, 2009, http://www.ynet.co.il/english/articles/0,7340,L-3754367,00 .html.

2. Philip Birnbaum, trans., *Daily Prayer Book: Ha-Siddur Ha-Shalem* (New York: Hebrew Publishing Company, 1977), Morning Service, 90.

3. I was greatly aided in my understanding of the temple layout by John W. Schmitt and J. Carl Laney, *Messiah's Coming Temple: Ezekiel's Prophetic Vision of the Future Temple* (Grand Rapids: Kregel, 1997).

Chapter 13 The Battle of Armageddon

1. B. W. Newton, *Expository Teaching on the Millennium and Israel's Future* (London: Collins, 1913), 161.

Part 6 The Coming Millennial Rule of Christ and the Arrival of the Eternal State

1. Nathaniel West, *The Thousand Years: Studies in Eschatology in Both Testaments* (1889; repr., Fincastle, VA: Scripture Truth, 1970). The foreword to this book was written by Wilbur Smith in its reprinting. He named the five scholars, all of whom were members of the Presbyterian Church except Peters. The five men were: Samuel H. Kellogg (1839–1899), professor at Western Theological Seminary; James H. Brookes (1830–1897), pastor in St. Louis; E. R. Craven (1824–1908), pastor of Third Presbyterian Church of Newark, NJ; George N. H. Peters (1825–1909) of the Evangelical Lutheran Church; and Nathaniel West (1826–1906), pastor of a number of Presbyterian churches.

Chapter 14 The Millennial Rule and Reign of God

1. Franz Delitzsch, *A Biblical Commentary on the Prophecies of Isaiah*, trans. James Martin (1884; repr., Grand Rapids: Eerdmans, 1954), 1:421.

2. See also Isaiah 3:1; 8:7; 10:33; 19:1; 22:17; 24:1; 26:21. Yet outside of Isaiah this attention-getting device is found only in Micah 1:3 and Amos 7:4.

Chapter 15 The New Creation

1. William R. Featherstone, "My Jesus, I Love Thee" (1864), in *Select Hymns (Timeless Truths)*, no. 292, v. 4 (1911), http://www.hymnary.org/text/my_jesus_i_love_thee_i_know _thou_art_mi.

Author Index

Subject Index

Scripture Index

Old Testament

Genesis
1:31 27
2:7 35
3:14 161
3:14–15 70
5:24 12
6:8 150
7:7 150
7:11 151
7:23 150
8:16 150
9:16 149
10 91
10:2 91
10:7 71
12:1–3 37, 38
12:2–3 72, 89, 156
12:2–4 23
12:3 75, 149
12:7 37, 38, 40, 89
15:1–6 25
15:18–21 40
16:10 38
16:11–12 87
17:7 149
17:7–8 40
17:7–9 38
17:8 156
17:13 149
17:19 149
18:13–14 24
18:14 35
18:18 72
19 94
22:2 54, 111

22:17–18 38, 72
25:8–10 3
26:3–4 72
28:4 38
28:13–14 72
28:13–15 38
37:35 4, 5
48:16 16
49:10 47

Exodus
13:20–21 60
14:21–31 49
15:3 136
15:13 17
23:16 80
23:31 70
32:34 xiii, xiv
34:22 80

Leviticus
11:24 12
11:44–45 138
19:31 12
20:6 12
20:14 4
20:27 12
23:33–44 140
25:1–7 104
25:18–19 26
25:23–25 16
25:25 21
25:47–55 16
26:4–8 26
26:6 26
26:40–42 48
27:28 107

Numbers
11:28 105
11:29 81
16:30 4, 5
19:11 12
35:19–27 16

Deuteronomy
5:26 17
6:5 28
10:16 26
16:10 80
16:13–15 140
18:10–11 12
28:1–14 161
30:6 26
32:39 14
33:3 138
33:28 26

Joshua
1:2 41
1:4 41
3:10 17
3:14–17 49
7:25 4
10:14 136
13:22 46
24:30 3
24:32 3

Judges
5:16 48
13:18 24

Ruth
4:4–15 16
4:10 16

1 Samuel
2:6 14
17:47 136
28:4–19 12
28:12 12
6:2 46
6:19 113

2 Samuel
3:32 3
6 54
7:13 69
7:16 69
7:19 149
14:11 16
15:30 136
22:6 5
23:3–4 70
23:5 149

1 Kings
10:1–13 72
10:14–15 71
16:11 16
17:17–24 13
17:22 14

2 Kings
4:29–37 13
13:17 47
13:21 13
17:23–24 84
21:6 12

1 Chronicles
1:5 91
13:9–10 113

181